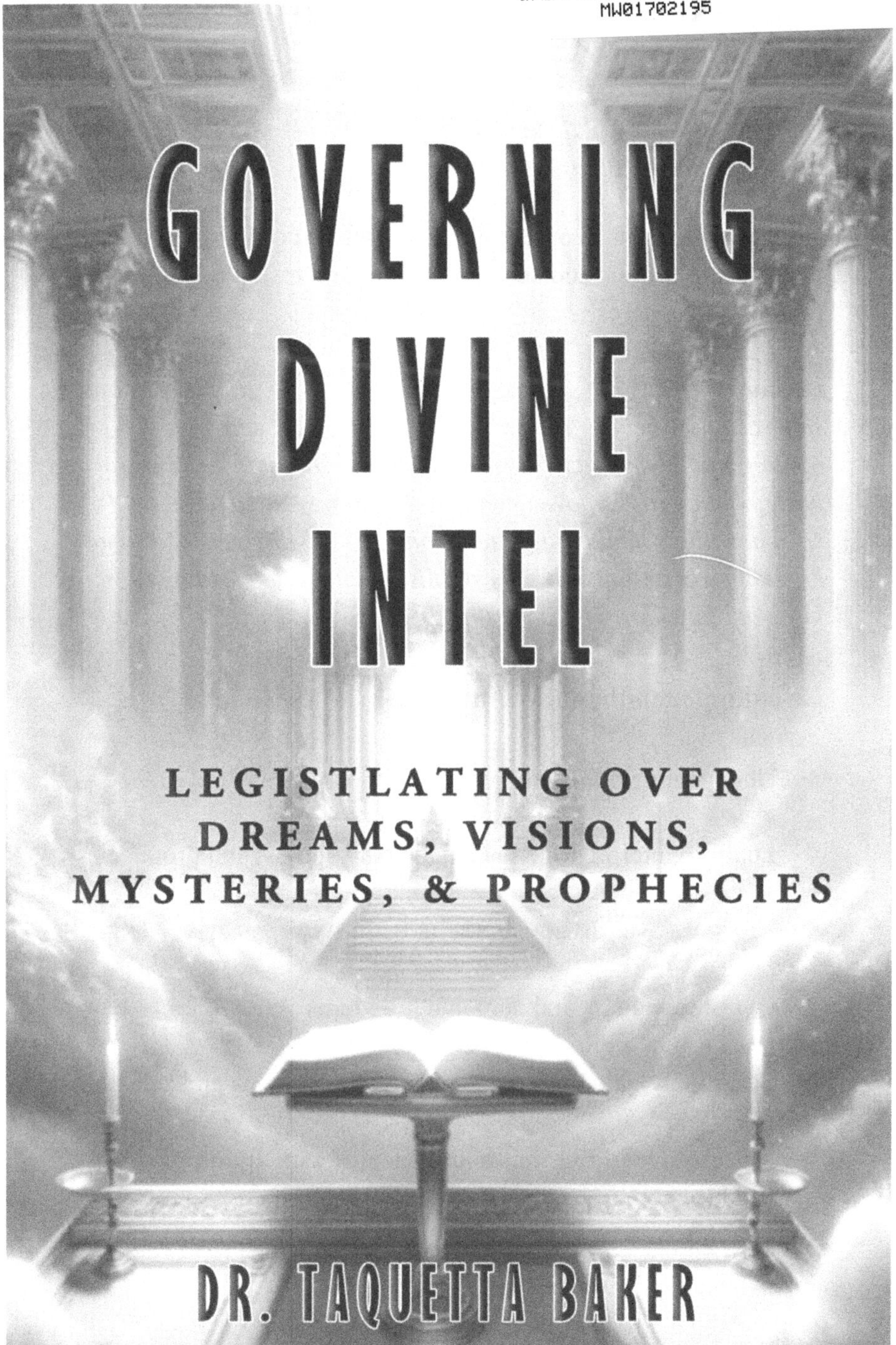

GOVERNING DIVINE INTEL

LEGISTLATING OVER DREAMS, VISIONS, MYSTERIES, & PROPHECIES

DR. TAQUETTA BAKER

Book Synopsis

Whoever owns the atmosphere, sea, the region, and the land, will rule and govern says the Lord.

God is wanting his people, especially fivefold officers, intercessory scouts, and seers, to govern and take jurisdiction in regions and spheres.

Do not just pray, but govern – claim your people, lands, regions, spheres of influence, and atmospheres by gatekeeping and owning the inheritance I have given you through them. Push back principalities, powers, rulers of darkness, and territorial spirits, while commanding and producing destiny purposes and kingdom works that SHIFT, establish, build, and sustain my kingdom in your midst, says the Lord.

Be equipped in the following areas:

- ❖ Understand your dominion and authority as a child of God
- ❖ Learn to interpret dreams, visions, mysteries, and prophecies
- ❖ Legislate over divine intel with maturity
- ❖ Overthrow altars and demonic kingdoms
- ❖ Effectively gate keep the people, lands, regions and spheres
- ❖ Release fivefold visions and mandates with divine success and kingdom impact

Kingdom Wellness Counseling and Mentoring Center

Christian Counseling

Ebook Products

Governing Divine Intel

Legislating Over Dreams, Visions, Mysteries, & Prophecies

Dr. TAQUETTA BAKER

Amazon Publications
Muncie, IN

Kingdom Wellness Counseling and Mentoring Center
Learning Applicable Destiny Equipping Tools

kingdomwellnesscenter@gmail.com

Kingdomshifters.com

KSWU.NET

Connect with Taquetta via Facebook or YouTube

TABLE OF CONTENTS

VISION STATEMENT

Kingdom Wellness offers a revolutionary theory of bridging mental and physical health with biblical truths, faith-based counseling, deliverance and healing principles. This is a holistic ideology of the total person – body, soul (mind, will, emotions), and spirit becoming one.

"Psychological theories are valuable for guiding practice in education, mental health, business, and other domains. They provide answers to intrinsically interesting questions concerning many kinds of thinking including perception, emotion, learning, and problem-solving."[i]

TAQUETTA BAKER, FOUNDER

As an adopted child, Taquetta knows the lifelong journey of appreciating both spiritual and natural relationships and encounters. She understands being strengthened by the pain that life can bring while embracing the joy of unexpected connections. Taquetta has transformed her experiences to establish a legacy of pioneering and fearlessly leading others.

Taquetta Baker is the founder of Kingdom Shifters Ministries (KSM), Kingdom Shifters Empowerment Church, and Kingdom Wellness Counseling and Mentoring Center. She has authored over 60 books and two prayer CD's. Taquetta has a Doctorate in Ministry, a Master's Degree in Community Counseling with an emphasis on Marriage, Children and Family Counseling, a Bachelor's Degree in Psychology and Associates Degree in Business Administration. Taquetta has a Therapon Belief Therapist Certification from the Therapon Institute, which provides faith-based counseling and ministry training. She is a certified Leadership & Executive Life Coach and has written her own Kingdom Wellness Counseling & Life Coaching theory and curriculum.

Taquetta serves in the mental health field as a Behavioral Consultant. She enjoys working with individuals and families who experience a broad range of psychological, emotional, social, relational, and spiritual challenges. Her outreach demonstrates cultural agility across a spectrum of ages, ethnicities, and socio-economic backgrounds. She is committed to empowering others with launching ministries, businesses, and books. She provides mentoring, counseling and vision launching through her Kingdom Wellness Counseling and Mentoring Center. With over 22 years of faith-based and professional counseling experience, her reputation is one who transforms lives and families through balancing biblical principles with applicable tools and strategies.

Taquetta serves on the Board of Directors for New Day Community Ministries, Inc. and is a graduate of the Eagles Dance Institute under Dr. Pamela Hardy with a license in liturgical dance. Before pioneering her own ministry, Taquetta was a dedicated member of Christ Temple Global Ministries for 14 years. She served pioneered Shekinah Expressions dance ministry and served in the role of prophet, teacher, presbytery board member, and overseer of the Altar Workers Ministry. Taquetta receives mentoring and ministry covering from Bishop Jackie Green, Founder of JGM-National Prayer Life Institute (Phoenix, AZ), and was ordained as an Apostle on June 7, 2014.

The Bible is full of stories that are centered around digging or receiving from wells which represent stability and deep places of renewal. Taquetta flows through the spiritual wells of warfare, worship, counseling and deliverance. Taquetta's mantle is an apostolic directive of judging and establishing God's kingdom in people, ministries, communities, and regions. Taquetta travels in foreign missions and throughout the United States. She has mentored and established dance teams, altar workers, counseling programs, and deliverance and prophetic ministries. Taquetta ministers in the areas of fine arts, systems of prayer, fivefold ministry, deliverance, healing, miracles, atmospheric worship, and counseling. Her mission is to empower and train others to identify and embrace their destiny.

Shift!

INTERPRETING DIVINE INTEL

I highly recommend these manuals I have scribed to further assist interpreting divine intel:

- *Let There Be Sight,*
- *Unmasking The Power Of The Scouts, Volume I*
- *Gatekeeping Regions For God's Glory*
- *Strategic Warfare Strategies For Prophets*
- *Ascending Into The Supernatural*
- *Fivefold Operations, Volume I*

Some of the revelation in this chapter are from these books.

Ephesians 1:17-23 *That the God of our Lord Jesus Christ, the Father of glory, may give unto you the spirit of wisdom and revelation in the knowledge of him: The eyes of your understanding being enlightened; that ye may know what is the hope of his calling, and what the riches of the glory of his inheritance in the saints, And what is the exceeding* *greatness of his power to us-ward who believe, according to the working of his mighty power, Which he wrought in Christ, when he raised him from the dead, and set him at his own right hand in the heavenly places, Far above all principality, and power, and might, and dominion, and every name that is named, not only in this world, but also in that which is to come: And hath put all things under his feet, and gave him to be the head over all things to the church, Which is his body, the fulness of him that filleth all in all.*

Enlightened is *phōtizō* in Greek and means:

1. to shine or (transitively) to brighten up (literally or figuratively
2. enlighten, illuminate, (bring to, give) light, make to see render evident
3. to cause something to exist and thus come to light and become clear to all
4. to spiritually, imbue with saving knowledge, to instruct
5. to inform, teach, to give understanding to, to discern

Divine enlightenment occurs in the following ways:

Dreams – A succession of experiences, stories, revelations, mysteries, inquiries, strategies, downloaded through ones spiritual and natural senses and the eyes of their understanding as they sleep. Dreams and night season visions involve real realms. Our body sleeps, but our spirit is eternal and never sleeps. Our spirit can engage God, heaven, spiritual realms, and if exposed, can even be subject to the enemy. This is the reason David says, in Psalms 91, that he dwells in the secret place of the Most

High. He understood the potential to engage the enemy while asleep. God loves to release intel via dreams and dream realms. It is important for scouts to not discount nightmarish type dreams as God could very well be revealing details. For more detailed insight in this area I recommend my book, "*Let There Be Sight.*"

The Spirit Of Wisdom – The Greek word for *wisdom* is *sophia* and means, "*broad and full of intelligence, the intimate understanding of God's word and purpose.*"

The Spirit Of Revelation – The Greek word for *revelation* is *apokalypsis* and means, "*disclosure, appearing, coming, lighten, manifestation, be revealed, make naked, make visible, disclose truth or instruction.*"

Gift of Discernment – This is the ability to yield a judicial estimation, distinguish, judge, dispute or discern between good and evil, particularly demonic forces.

Seer Vision – God given, God driven, God ordained mental images, pictures, daydreams, trances, revealed through a supernatural seer lance that conveys revelation or intel. God will allow the eyes of a prophet's imagination and understanding to be opened and empowered so they can peer into someone's life, ministry, business, situation, or region, to see what is or will occur, and how to aide them in present and future maters. He may give the prophet pictures, images, play by play, a spiritual tour, or full visions. God guides the prophet in this. They do not open these portals independent of God as this exposes the prophet to what is called a "third eye" where they are receiving information illegally and through demonic assistance. The eyes of a prophet's understanding are a part of their spirit and thus what is being filtered into their imagination is from God's spirit to their spirit.

> ***2Corinthians 12:1-7*** *It is not expedient for me doubtless to glory. I will come to visions and revelations of the Lord. I knew a man in Christ above fourteen years ago, (whether in the body, I cannot tell; or whether out of the body, I cannot tell: God knoweth;) such an one caught up to the third heaven. And I knew such a man, (whether in the body, or out of the body, I cannot tell: God knoweth;) How that he was caught up into paradise, and heard unspeakable words, which it is not lawful for a man to utter. Of such an one will I glory: yet of myself I will not glory, but in mine infirmities. For though I would desire to glory, I shall not be a fool; for I will say the truth: but now I forbear, lest any man should think of me above that which he seeth me to be, or that he heareth of me.*

Translations – Via prayer, dreams, and vision, God will translate a prophet in the spirit to different realms and spheres of heaven, demonic realms, unknown or hidden realms, spiritual high places, worldly realms and spheres to gain entail regarding worldly and witchcraft activities, demons and demonic systems, and other insight needed to help guide, warn, equip, and navigate people, lands, regions, and spheres.

Mysteries & Revelations – Mysteries and revaluations are supernatural intel that God reveals to those he trusts and deem as friends. These mysteries include secret spiritual keys, strategies, truths, foolish insights that bring deliverance, healing, breakthrough, freedom, elevation, provision to God's people, lands, regions, spheres, and nations. As a friend of God, you are privy to heavenly visions, wisdom, revelation, knowledge, counsel, might, judgements, justice, translations, the literal kingdom of heaven, storehouses, weaponry, and provision.

> ***Matthew 13:10-11*** *And the disciples came, and said unto him, Why speakest thou unto them in parables? He answered and said unto them, Because it is given unto you to know the mysteries of the kingdom of heaven, but to them it is not given.*
>
> ***Ephesians 1:9*** *He made known to us the mystery of His will, according to His kind intention which He purposed in Him.*
>
> ***Luke 2:8*** *And He said, "To you it has been granted to know the mysteries of the kingdom of God, but to the rest it is in parables, so that seeing they may not see, and hearing they may not understand.*
>
> ***1Corinthians 2:10*** *For to us God revealed them through the Spirit; for the Spirit searches all things, even the depths of God.*
>
> ***1Corinthians 2:9*** *But just as it is written, "Things which eye has not seen and ear has not heard, And*

which have not entered the heart of man, All that God has prepared for those who love Him.

Sevenfold Spirit Of The Lord - Manifold spirit and power graces of the Holy Spirit that can rest upon us to reveal mysteries and revelation.

Isaiah 11:2 *And the spirit of the Lord shall rest upon him, the spirit of wisdom and understanding, the spirit of counsel and might, the spirit of knowledge and of the fear of the Lord.*

The Spirit Of The Lord – The spirit of the Lord is the Holy Spirit upon us that operates as God's supernatural power to create and produce grace, sufficiency, miracles, signs, and wonders.

The Spirit Of Wisdom - The natural and/or spiritual ability to understand things that other people cannot understand or do not have the knowledge of. They possess a perspective of what is proper, reasonable, good sense or balanced judgment. Those who have the gift of wisdom have the experience, gift of common sense, enlightenment, clear thinking, foresight, perception, brains, sanity, or stability of God released to enlighten, empower, and advance people, situations, lands, atmospheres, and regions.

The Spirit Of Understanding - To perceive the meaning of, grasp the idea of, comprehend, connect the insights, or provide clarity to what God is speaking or what is being revealed.

The Spirit Of Counseling - To perceive the meaning of, grasp the idea of, comprehend, connect the insights, or provide clarity to what God is speaking or what is being revealed. Counseling is not advice. It is a committed process to wholeness whether by entering a counseling process or receiving counsel and then utilizing the revelation to navigate to an end goal.

The Spirit Of Might – To possess supernatural force, power, strength, ability, and capability beyond one's natural means in order to be brave, courageous, warlike, enduring and persevering in challenging times.

The Spirit Of Knowledge - Facts, information, understanding, or the state of being aware of something about a person or situation via the Holy Spirit. One with this gift can also exemplify knowledge beyond their years or natural understanding. They have no means of proving what they know other than by the Holy Spirit and the confirmation of others.

The Fear of The Lord – To possess an unrelenting love, honor, reverence, and awe for the Lord with a desire to serve Him, worship Him, be obedient to

Him, please Him, and live in covenant with Him as a lifestyle.

Prophecies - Prophecy means to edify, comfort, and exhort a person or body of people; testifies of the goodness of Jesus. Though the releaser may provide past and present knowledge, the prophecy provides foresight into the future. If there is no foresight, it is not a prophecy. If a person is in the Office of a Prophet, they can judge, rebuke, correct, direct, display the anger of the Lord to a people, region, or nation.

> *Prophecy* in Greek is *prophēteia* and means "*prediction (scriptural or other), a discourse emanating from divine inspiration and declaring the purposes of God, whether by reproving and admonishing the wicked, or comforting the afflicted, or revealing things hidden; esp. by foretelling future events.*"

Prophet in the Strong's Concordance means:
1. Inspired man
2. Spokesman
3. Speaker

Seer in the Strong's Concordance means:
1. A beholder in vision
2. Stargazer
3. Prophet
4. Vision

2Kings 17:13 New Living Bible *Again and again the Lord had sent his prophets and seers to warn both Israel and Judah: "Turn from all your evil ways. Obey my commands and decrees—the entire law that I commanded your ancestors to obey, and that I gave you through my servants the prophets."*

Interpreting Divine Intel

Do not fear or be insecure about interpreting your intel. Fear and insecurity clog your ability to hear and receive interpretation and direction from God. Trust that since God is allowing the intel, he will provide an interpretation for it. God will tell you what is for now and what is for later. He will reveal what to do with what he shares. Remember it is his intel not yours. Be lead of him regarding it. You want to honor and reverence him in humility for his willingness to use you as a conduit of his intel.

Write down or record the dream, vision, mystery, revelation, prophecy immediately. This will help you to retain as much intel as possible. If you do not have time to write it down, record it using the audio memo on your phone or other device. Make time to go back and journal the dream as it is easier to identify insights when you engrave them.

Habakkuk 2:2 *And the Lord answered me: "Write the vision; make it plain on tablets, so he may run who reads it.*

Do not neglect journaling your dreams, visions, mysteries, revelations, prophecies. People will try to recall dreams days, months, years later and only can recall a measure of the intel. Or they replace parts of the dream with information that may not be the truth of what was downloaded to them. This is dangerous, lazy, unwise, and is disregarding of what God is privying. This lack of governance reveals your heart posture in being able to adequately govern and honor what God speaks and reveals to you. If you really care you would steward the intel well. This also dims your ability to steward your life, regions, spheres, and lives God has granted to your hands. You spend unnecessary time asking God for revelation, praying, interceding, and waring in areas that God may have already provided direction to you about.

Sometimes God will hide intel in your heart for the future so he may not give an immediate interpretation, allot only partial revelation, or cause you to remember only portions of the intel. , If you fail to record what he does give, then when he awakens what has been hidden, you are not able to partner with his mysteries and will for this present season it is needed.

1Corinthians 13:9-13 *For we know in part, and we prophesy in part. But when that which is perfect is come, then that which is in part shall be done away. When I was a child, I spake as a child, I understood as a child, I thought as a child: but when I became a man, I put away childish things. For now we see through a glass, darkly; but then face to face: now I know in part; but then shall I know even* *as also I am known. And now abideth faith, hope, charity, these three; but the greatest of these is charity.*

Exodus 23:30 *Little by little I will drive them out before you, until you have increased enough to take possession of the land.*

Even if the intel presents as demonic or soulish, write it down. There are key insights in these experiences as well. Search them out with the Lord and ask him to reveal intel to you regarding the demonic realm, demonic systems, and operations; or areas your soul that may need deliverance, healing, or maturity.

Do not assume intel that includes, demons, creatures, witches, warlocks, witchcraft activities, etc. are not of God. Many prophets and seers in the Bible had some wild, strange, fearful encounters that revealed heavenly realms, spiritual beings from heaven, spiritual regions and spheres, spiritual wickedness in high places, judgments, warnings, demonic insights, the heart and souls of the people, etc. Search the revelation out with God and allow him to reveal if the intel is from him or not. And even then, ask him to share intel regarding what you experience. This can help you close down realms and spheres that God may not want you to tread in. Or it can reveal your jurisdiction, governance, and legislation in supernatural territories and terrains.

Ephesians 6:12 *For we wrestle not against flesh and blood, but against principalities, against powers, against* *the rulers of the darkness of this world, against spiritual wickedness in high places.*

High is *epouranios* in the Greek and means:

1. above the sky, celestial, heavenly, high
2. existing in the heaven, things that take place in the heaven
3. the heavenly regions
    a. heaven itself, the abode of God and angels
    b. the lower heavens, of the stars,
    c. the heavens, of the clouds
4. the heavenly temple or sanctuary
5. of heavenly origin or nature

Factors to consider when interpreting intel:

- Colors
- Numbers, Symbols, Addresses, Phone Numbers, Blueprints
- Thoughts, Feelings, Emotions
- Spiritual and Natural Senses Being Impacted (Touch, Taste, Smell, Hearing, Sight, Will)
- Weather – Rain, Shine, Sleet, Snow, Tornados, Cyclones, Hurricanes, Tsumanis, Volcanoes
- Time of day – Morning, Noon, Midday, Afternoon, Night
- Spiritual Watches – 12am to 3am, 3am to 6am, 6am to 9pm, 9pm to 12pm

- Seasons – Winter, Spring, Summer, Fall
- Past, Present, Future
- Conception, In The Womb, Childhood, Teenage Years, Adulthood, Middle Age, Old Age, Death, After Life
- Generational Lineages – Ancient Times, Slave Times, Mother's or Father's Household/Bloodline
- Before Christ, After Christ
- Mobile, Stationary, Parked, Walking, Flying, Runing, Soaring, Jumping
- Cars, Trucks, Jeeps, Tractors And Equipment, Planes, Motor Cycles, Bikes, Scooters, Skates
- Locations & Places
- Buildings, Stores, Houses, Agencies, Marketplace Areas, Brothels, Hospitals, Schools, Colleges, Universities
- Internet Realms, Social Media Platforms,
- Highways, Roads, Streets, Dirt Roads
- Land, Water, Mountains, Valleys, Terrains, Skys, Desserts, Forests
- Sun, Moon, Starts, Constellations, Galaxies, Universe, Elements
- Communities, Neighborhoods, Cities, States, Regions, Spheres Of Influence, Nations
- Spiritual Realms Versus Natural Realms

- Kingdom Of Heaven Versus Demonic Realms, Regions, Kingdoms
- Death, Hell, Grave, Coffins
- Is God In The Intel – Father, Son, Holy Spirit, Representative of God, Scriptures, Scrolls, The Bible, Prayer Shawls, Christian Apparel
- Godly Acts, Tabernacle, Holies Of Holies, Churches, Temples, Ministries, Services, Conferences, Stages, Platforms, Court Of Heaven, Storehouses Of heaven
- Is Satan Or Demons In The Intel – Demonic Agents, Principalities, Powers, Territorial Spirits, Witches, Warlocks, Demonic And Wicked People, Familiar Spirits, Shapeshifters
- Witchcraft And Idolatrous Practices, Covens, Altars, Trading Floors, Dedicated Sites, Thrones, Shrines
- Carnal And Worldly Acts, Sin Issues, Propensities, Character Flaws, Forms Of Godliness, Angels Of Light, Truth Bearering, Iniquities, Transgressions, Curses, Dedications, Covenants
- People In The Intel; Who And What They Repesent; What Are Their Names, Postitions In Your Life And In The Intel– Family, Friends, Acquaintances, Strangers, Crowds Of People, Males, Females, Good People, Bad People, Indifferent People

- Ethnicities, Races, Personality Types, Culture Trends & Factors Regarding People & Systems In The Intel
- Occupations And Roles Of The People In The Intel
- Operations Behind The People In The Intel, Motives, Purposes
- What Is Occuring
- What Was Said, How Was It Said, Who Said What, Where Was It Said
- What Is The Dream About
- How Are You And Others Being Impacted
- What Are You And Others Experiencing As The intel Is Being Revealed
- What Are The Key Actions And Operations In the Intel
- Are You Watching, Participating, A Common Factor In The Intel
- Did You Dream, Have A Vision, Experience A Translation, Receive Download In Prayer; Received Intel While Studying The Bible, Journaling, Praise And Worship, Resting With God, On The Go; Received A Download As You Slept, Was Listening To A Sermon Or Teaching, Etc.
- Is It A Parable – A Short Story Designed To Illustate Or Teach Truth, Godly Principle, A Moral Lesson

- Deliverance, Healing, Breakthrough, Freedom, Evangelism, Salvation, Destiny Moment, Destiny Evolving, Transitions, Success, Advancement
- Warning, Repentence, Turning From Sin And Wickedness, Exposure, Judgments, Famines, Pestilances, Curses, Justices, Restoration, Restitution, Ourpouring, Harvesst, Blessings

Though not always the case, colors can be a representation of the following:

The definitions below were acquired from the article entitled, "*Prophetic Dance,*" by Apostle Pamela Hardy.

- Gold – The Deity of Christ (One of the Colors of the Tabernacle, ***Exodus 28***)
- Silver – Redemption
- Bronze – Refinement
- Black – Death, Famine, Peril
- Green – Everlasting Life, Prosperity
- Purple - Royalty
- Scarlet – The Passion of Christ, His Humanity
- Blue – Heavenly Things, Refreshing River, Holy Spirit
- Red – The blood of Jesus
- Rainbow – Covenant
- White – Holiness, Purity, Light, Righteousness

Ask God to make sure your interpretation of colors in alignment with what is being revealed. Do not interpret without God. Avoid using dream interpretation books if possible. If Holy Spirit does not highlight factors in the dream, then just journal the intel and wait for his interpretation. Ask an experience person who possess the gift of dream interpretion. Take what they share back to God before deeming it of him.

When I am interpreting intel, I operate through my scout and seer vision. Therefore, I ask God if is:

- ✓ **Onefold**: Just about me and the people or situations in the intel?

- ✓ **Twofold**: Revelation for my sphere of influence - ministries, businesses, organizations, team, divine assignment?

- ✓ **Threefold**: For the body of Christ?

I interp the intel from these three dimensions or from oneor two dimensions that he is showing me they are for. This means you can sometimes have one to three different interpretations of what God is speaking, what he is saying to you, what he is saying to you and those in the dream, what he is saying to the body of Christ. Seek to interpret from all three dimensions. Do not as assume that he is revealing the same intel in every dimension. Seek him for exactly what he is downloading what what he wants you to do with the revelation.

I also want to say that just because the people are in the intel does not mean God wants you to share it with them or implement what is in the intel. I only share with those in the intel as God leads. I also search out what is symbolism and what is for activation.

Sometimes, the people seen in the intel can be shapeshifters, familiar spirits, or astral projectors.

- **Shapeshifters** are demons that can change their form to appear as any person living, dead, or fictional. Initially, shapeshifters appear harmless (cats turning into lions and attacking) or even look like someone you know. It will then turn into a demon or evil thing in the dream and attack you. Shapeshifters are very subtly in dreams and tend to attack when they get you to a place of trusting them or thinking you are safe and have no reason to be alarmed. Be discerning as shapeshifters will attempt to draw you to places in a dream where you will be harmed, attacked, or all of a sudden you are being chased and running for your life.

- **Familiar Spirits** that work in dreams and visions look like someone you know, but really are demons. Though familiar spirits will look and sound familiar, they will not have the character or personality of the person you know, will not act the way the person would normally act. They will be trying to get you to do things that are contrary to God or to what is for you and will not be for you in the dream.

- **Astral Projectors** tend to be witches, warlocks, or regular people who separate their soul from their physical bodies so they can travel around the heavenly realms. Though demons can attack you sexually at night, sometimes these attacks are astral projectors. They are real people translating themselves into the spirit realm to rape and molest people. They do this for thrills or just because, or to feed an altar or satanic power. Sometimes, when people have encounters in their home where they see shadows, figures of people, or things moving around, these are not always what we call ghosts or demonic entities. Astral Projectors love to scare and play tricks on people. They are thrill seekers at the expense of the general public who like to act as if these types of experiences only occur in movies. As you become keener in discernment and being interactive in your dreams, you will be able to discern whether you are dealing with demons or astral projectors. Most astral projectors will flee if you threaten to cut their silver cord. The cord is what connects their soul to their body, and they can literally die if they are disconnected from it. They also flee from rebukes in Jesus' name and the blood of Jesus. If they do not respond to a rebuke or threat of cutting their cord, they are most likely a ghost or a territorial spirit that has some connection to that region or place. This would require a cleansing of the land and building to rid of these attacks.

Ecclesiastes 12:5-7 *Also when they shall be afraid of that which is high, and fears shall be in the way, and the almond tree shall flourish, and the grasshopper shall be a burden, and desire shall fail: because man goeth to his long home, and the mourners go about the* *streets: Or ever the silver cord be loosed, or the golden bowl be broken, or the pitcher be broken at the fountain, or the wheel broken at the cistern. Then shall the dust return to the earth as it was: and the spirit shall return unto God who gave it.*

- **Witch (female sorceress) - Warlock (male sorcerer)** - Witches and warlocks tend to release their spells and attacks in the night. They use translation and astral projection to enter the heavenlies to work their spells and bind people. You may encounter a witch or warlock when God leads you to go into the heavenlies to intercede and pray. Witches and warlocks will immediately attack you when they see you. They are territorial and will attempt to assert authority over their sphere of influence. They will see the light of God in you and assume you are there to judge them or overtake their sphere. They will attack in an effort to protect themselves. Some witches and warlocks will repent and even give their life to God. Some will be sold out to the devil and will stand their ground and fight. Ask God to lead you in how to deal with witches and warlocks.

  - God may have you cast them out of the heavenlies.
  - God may have you physically fight them.
  - God may tell you to have them repent and give their life to Him as He may want to use them for the kingdom.
  - God may tell you to have them decide whether they choose to repent or die as in the bible God has little

tolerance for witches and warlocks – "***Exodus 2:18*** *18 Thou shalt not suffer a witch to live.*" Some witches and warlocks are sold out for Satan and will choose death because they will refuse to repent. Be sensitive to what God is leading you to do and do not be afraid - for greater is God's power in you than in them.

Sometimes people we know in our intel are being used so that we will pay attention to what God is revealing. So do not always assume that they are shapeshifters or familiar spirits. Ask God to reveal to you if this is the case, the intel is about them, or they are being used by him for a specific purpose.

When sharing your intel, only share what God is requiring. Leave out the names of those in the dream unless God say otherwise. Sometimes, God will have you share in a manner to protect whatever intel he wants to reveal. I never go pass the scope of God. This is vital to your hearers being able to receive what God is saying as that is the key. What is God saying versus what you want to share through your heart for the people he wants to share it with or your motives in sharing (e.i. self-validation,'vengeance, immaturity, righteous indignation, etc.).

Sometimes, our audience cannot handle the details of the intel or even how we received it. Sometimes they will get caught up in the supernatural experiences we have encountered and mess the entire message God is revealing. Sometimes, the intel can be so creepy they have a difficult time receiving so it is best to leave that part out and share the key revelation from the experience or intel.

Ask God for scriptural revelation to confirm and parallel what is being revealed in your intel. Scriptural revelation will solidify your intel and infuse it with power to manifest what God is desiring.

Seek God for the proceeding word, goals, strategies, guidance, and direction to the intel. Be obedient to what he is speaking. Encourage obedience of others to which the intel is being shared. Govern the intel by holding yourself and others accountable. But also, be mindful that people have freewill. Do not attempt to override their freewill. If they are not regarding of the intel, ask God how to interceed or assist them. If he does not lead you to do another, then allow him to deal with them. If he does lead you to lead or assist the, be obedient. Much of the time, God will require you to interceed rather than keep confronting a person. Give people time to search out the intel and God for themselves. Governing is not about controlling, punishing, or demanding people regard what your intel. Governing is about trusting God and the dominon he has given you to legitimate his word, will, purpose, and kingdom for his glory. He will perform and perfect everything he reveals to you. Let him defend and show forth his great glory in his timing and his way.

Jeremiah 1:12 ***The Amplified Bible*** *"Then said the Lord to me, You have seen well, for I am alert and active, watching over My word to perform it."*

Ezekiel 12:25 The Amplified Bible *For I am the Lord; I will speak, and the word that I shall speak shall be performed (come to pass); It will no longer be delayed, for in your days, O rebellious house, I will speak the word and I will fulfill it," says the Lord GOD.*

GOVERNING OVER DIVINE INTEL

STUDY THE SCRIPTURES IN THIS MANUAL. DO NOT SKIP OVER THEM! BUILD YOURSELF IN THE POWER OF BIBLICAL TRUTH REGARDING THIS REVELATION, AS IT WILL GROUND YOU AND POSTURE YOU FOR GREATER KINGDOM INTEL!

Shift!

Intel Scriptures - God releases divine intel for the purposes of rebuke, correction, chastisement, warning, judgement, exposure, deliverance, healing, breakthrough, salvation, reconciliation, restoration, insight, hindsight, foresight, vision, clarity, knowledge, understanding, enlightenment, truth, strategies, goals, and obedience to his plans and purposes.

Isaiah 11:2 *And the spirit of the Lord shall rest upon him, the spirit of wisdom and understanding, the spirit of counsel and might, the spirit of knowledge and of the fear of the Lord.*

Jeremiah 33:3 *Call to Me and I will answer you, and I will tell you great and mighty things, which you do not know.*

Deuteronomy 29:29 *The secret things belong unto the LORD our God: but those things which are revealed belong unto us and to our children for ever, that we may do all the words of this law.*

Ephesians 1:9 *He made known to us the mystery of His will, according to His kind intention which He purposed in Him.*

Luke 2:8 *And He said, "To you it has been granted to know the mysteries of the kingdom of God, but to the rest it is in parables, so that seeing they may not see, and hearing they may not understand."*

1Corinthians 2:10 *For to us God revealed them through the Spirit; for the Spirit searches all things, even the depths of God.*

1Corinthians 2:9 *But just as it is written, "Things which eye has not seen and ear has not heard, And which have not entered the heart of man, All that God has prepared for those who love Him."*

Psalm 64:6 *They devise injustices, saying, "We are ready with a well-conceived plot;" For the inward thought and the heart of a man are deep.*

Job 38:16-17 *"Have you entered into the springs of the sea or walked in the recesses of the deep? "Have the gates of death been revealed to you, or have you seen the gates of deep darkness?*

Romans 11:33-36 *O the depth of the riches both of the wisdom and knowledge of God! how unsearchable are his judgments, and his ways past finding out! For who hath known the mind of the Lord? or who hath been his counsellor? Or who hath first given to him, and it shall be recompensed unto him again? For of him, and through him, and to him, are all things: to whom be glory for ever. Amen.*

Governing Through Sonship

It is not enough, especially in this day and hour, to just pray over lands, people, regions, atmospheres, situations, experiences, frequencies, and airways. As we pray and gatekeep, we must LITERALLY claim jurisdiction, spiritually govern, and assert our right as dominion legislators in these areas. We must take up spiritual residence and governance in and over those terrains so that the enemy and all connected to him cannot claim it, or rule and inhabit there. We must assert authority and establish that this terrain and ALL within it belongs to God and to us as his people.

Genesis 1:28 *And God blessed them, and God said unto them, Be fruitful, and multiply, and replenish the earth, and subdue it: and have dominion over the fish of the sea, and the fowl of the air, and over every living thing that moveth upon the earth.*

Deuteronomy 15:6 New King James Bible *For the LORD your God will bless you just as He promised you; you shall lend to many nations, but you shall not borrow; you shall reign over many nations, but they shall not reign over you.*

Deuteronomy 28:12 *You shall lend to many nations, but you shall not borrow. The Lord will open for you His good store-house, the heavens. He will give rain to your land*

Psalm 2:7-12 *I will declare the decree: the LORD hath said unto me, Thou art my Son; this day have I begotten thee. Ask of me, and I shall give thee the heathen for thine inheritance, and the uttermost parts of the earth for thy possession. Thou shalt break them with a rod of iron; thou shalt dash them in pieces like a potter's vessel. Be wise now therefore, O ye kings: be instructed, ye judges of the earth. Serve the LORD with fear, and rejoice with* *trembling. Kiss the Son, lest he be angry, and ye perish from the way, when his wrath is kindled but a little.*

Psalm 18:43-49 *Thou hast delivered me from the strivings of the people; and thou hast made me the head of the heathen: a people whom I have not known shall serve me. As soon as they hear of me, they shall obey me: the strangers shall submit themselves unto me. The strangers shall fade away, and be afraid out of their close places. The LORD liveth; and blessed be my rock; and let the God of my salvation be exalted. It is God that avengeth me, and subdueth the people under me. He delivereth me from mine enemies: yea, thou liftest me up above those that rise up against me: thou hast delivered me from the violent man.*

Job 25:2 *Dominion and fear belong to Him; He makes peace in His high places.*

Psalm 8:6 *You have made him to have dominion over the works of Your hands; You have put all things under his feet.*

Psalm 19:13 *Keep back Your servant also from presumptuous sins; let them not have dominion over me.*

Psalm 49:14 *Like sheep they are laid in the grave; death shall feed on them; the upright shall have dominion over them in the morning; and their beauty shall be consumed in the grave, far from their dwelling.*

Psalm 72:8 *He shall have dominion also from sea to sea, and from the River to the ends of the earth.*

Psalm 119:133 *Direct my steps by Your word, and let no iniquity have dominion over me.*

Judges 5:13 *Then he made him that remaineth have dominion over the nobles among the people: the LORD made me have dominion over the mighty.*

Romans 6:9 *Knowing that Christ, having been raised from the dead, dies no more. Death no longer has dominion over Him.*

Romans 6:14 *For sin shall not have dominion over you, for you are not under law but under grace.*

Ephesians 1:17-21 *That the God of our Lord Jesus Christ, the Father of glory, may give to you the spirit of wisdom and revelation in the knowledge of Him, the eyes of your understanding being enlightened; that you may know what is the hope of His calling, what are the riches of the glory of His inheritance in the saints, and what is the exceeding greatness of His power toward us who believe, according to the working of His mighty power which He worked in Christ when He raised Him from the dead and seated Him at His right hand in the heavenly places, far above all principality and power and might and dominion, and every name that is named, not only in this age but also in that which is to come.*

1Peter 5:11 *To him be glory and dominion for ever and ever. Amen.*

Colossians 2:13-15 *And you, being dead in your sins and the uncircumcision of your flesh, hath he quickened together with him, having forgiven you all trespasses; Blotting out the handwriting of ordinances that was against* *us, which was contrary to us, and took it out of the way, nailing it to his cross; And having spoiled principalities and powers, he made a shew of them openly, triumphing over them in it.*

New International Bible *When you were dead in your sins and in the uncircumcision of your flesh, God made you alive with Christ. He forgave us all our sins, having canceled the charge of our legal indebtedness, which stood against us and condemned us; he has taken it away, nailing it to the cross. And having disarmed the powers and authorities, he made a public spectacle of them, triumphing over them by the cross.*

Know Your Metrons & Jurisdiction – Even as you assert dominion via sonship, it is important to understand your sphere of influence.

Dictionary.com defines jurisidiction as:

1. the right, power, or authority to administer justice by hearing and determining controversies
3. power; authority; control
4. the extent or range of judicial, law enforcement, or other authority
5. the territory over which authority is exercised

Mark 16:15 *And he said unto them, Go ye into all the world, and preach the gospel to every creature.*

Acts 1:18 *But ye shall receive power, after that the Holy Ghost is come upon you: and ye shall be witnesses unto me* *both in Jerusalem, and in all Judaea, and in Samaria, and unto the uttermost part of the earth.*

2Corinthians 10:13-16 The Amplified Bible *We, on the other hand, will not boast beyond our legitimate province and proper limit, but will keep within the limits [of our commission which] God has allotted us as our measuring line and which reaches and includes even you. For we are not overstepping the limits of our province and stretching beyond our ability to reach, as though we reached not (had no legitimate mission) to you, for we were [the very first] to come even as far as to you with the good news (the Gospel) of Christ. We do not boast therefore, beyond our proper limit, over other men's labors, but we have the hope and confident expectation that as your faith continues to grow, our field among you may be greatly enlarged, still within the limits of our commission, so that [we may even] preach the Gospel in lands [lying] beyond you, without making a boast of work already done in another [man's] sphere of activity [before we came on the scene].*

Romans 12:3-6 The Amplified Bible *For by the grace [of God] given to me I say to everyone of you not to think more highly of himself [and of his importance and ability] than he ought to think; but to think so as to have sound judgment, as God has apportioned to each a degree of faith [and a purpose designed for service]. For just as in one [physical] body we have many parts, and these parts do not all have the same function or special use, so we, who are many, are [nevertheless just] one body in Christ, and individually [we are] parts one of another [mutually* *dependent on each other]. Since we have gifts that differ according to the grace given to us, each of us is to use them accordingly…*

Measure in the Greek is *Metron* and means: '*a determined quantity, extent, portion measured off, measure or limit,' limited measure, or, in other words, jurisdiction*, a sphere of authority, anointing, calling, purpose, and influence.

Though we are called to go into all the earth to witness, evangelize, and win souls, we have a specific remember and sphere we are to govern through our sonship in God. We have a unique identity of God on the inside of us that is to impact the earth strategically, specifically, and necessarily. This is the reason relationship with God is so important. Through relationship and constant abiding in him, we are able to learn our unique God identity and how to legislate it in the earth. This also helps us to honor who each of us are in God and work together so that the different facets of who God is on the inside of us can unify for a greater kingdom impact.

When operating in your metron aka jurisdiction, it is important to:

- Recognize, claim, and govern that your metron God has given you.
- Understand that God governs the timing and seasons to which your metron is released.
- Know by God's direction when you are to have global impact, when to expand into greater

dimensions of your metron over times and seasons. Also, spiritually mapping these areas so you know how to properly war, legislate, and govern authority over principalities, powers, laws, governmental systems.

- Know when and how to pray, plant, release, plow, cultivate, the visions and intel God has and will provide.
- Know that your remnant, land, seas, communities, regions, nations, spheres of influence need who you are in God. They need your unique God identity. They need you personally and the rest of the believers in your sphere need you so they can connect to advance and expand the kingdom of God for his glory.

Legislating Over Demons

As you are governing and laying claim, legislation over demonic spirits, systems, and operations is essential for pushing back, dismantling, nullifying, and overthrowing principalities, rulers, powers, territorial spirits, and spiritual wickedness in high places. Command them to leave and for any hidden agendas to be thwarted in Jesus' name.

Ephesians 6:12-13 *For we wrestle not against flesh and blood, but against principalities, against powers, against the rulers of the darkness of this world, against spiritual wickedness in high places. Wherefore take unto you the whole armour of God, that ye may be able to withstand in the evil day, and having done all, to stand. Stand therefore, having your loins girt about with truth, and having on the breastplate of righteousness; And your feet shod with the* *preparation of the gospel of peace; Above all, taking the shield of faith, wherewith ye shall be able to quench all the fiery darts of the wicked. And take the helmet of salvation, and the sword of the Spirit, which is the word of God: Praying always with all prayer and supplication in the Spirit, and watching thereunto with all perseverance and supplication for all saints.*

Luke 10:19 *Behold, I have given you authority to tread on serpents and scorpions, and over all the power of the enemy, and nothing shall hurt you.*

Romans 8:37-39 *We more than conquerors through him that loved us. For I am persuaded, that neither death, nor life, nor angels, nor principalities, nor powers, nor things present, nor things to come, Nor height, nor depth, nor any other creature, shall be able to separate us from the love of God, which is in Christ Jesus our Lord.*

Legislating Revelation

It is also not enough to just talk about and share dreams, visions, enlightenments, mysteries, prophecies, words of revelation and knowledge especially those that present as rebukes, reproof, chastisements, exposure, warnings, judgments, calamities, etc. We must govern over what God is revealing or allowing us to have privy to and seek him regarding what to do with this intel. We need to know if we should be:

- Interceding to cancel what we are being enlightened about.

- Seeking his forgiveness, grace, and mercy, such that repentance and turning will fall upon the guilty and they would turn from their wicked ways or position ourselves where he grants grace and relinquishes judgment because our intercession holds back judgment.

2Chronicles 7:14 *If my people, which are called by my name, shall humble themselves, and pray, and seek my face, and turn from their wicked ways; then will I hear from heaven, and will forgive their sin, and will heal their land.*

Habbukak 2:1-3 *I will stand upon my watch, and set me upon the tower, and will watch to see what he will say unto me, and what I shall answer when I am reproved. And the LORD answered me, and said, Write the vision, and make it plain upon tables, that he may run that readeth it. For the vision is yet for an appointed time, but at the end it shall speak, and not lie: though it tarry, wait for it; because it will surely come, it will not tarry.*

Abraham was a great example of interceding for people after being given insight on judgement concerning them.

Genesis 18:20-29 *And the LORD said, Because the cry of Sodom and Gomorrah is great, and because their sin is very grievous; I will go down now, and see whether they have done altogether according to the cry of it, which is come unto me; and if not, I will know. And the men turned their faces from thence, and went toward Sodom: but Abraham* ***stood*** *yet before the LORD. And Abraham drew near, and said, Wilt thou also destroy the righteous with the* *wicked? Peradventure there be fifty righteous within the city: wilt thou also destroy and not spare the place for the fifty righteous that are therein? That be far from thee to do after this manner, to slay the righteous with the wicked: and that the righteous should be as the wicked, that be far from thee: Shall not the Judge of all the earth do right? And the LORD said, If I find in Sodom fifty righteous within the city, then I will spare all the place for their sakes. And Abraham answered and said, Behold now, I have taken upon me to speak unto the Lord, which am but dust and ashes: Peradventure there shall lack five of the fifty righteous: wilt thou destroy all the city for lack of five? And he said, If I find there forty and five, I will not destroy it. And he spake unto him yet again, and said, Peradventure there shall be forty found there. And he said, I will not do it for forty's sake.*

The scripture says Abraham STOOD before the Lord. While standing, he inquired of God's plans and interceded on behalf of the judgment God revealed. He did not say, "*Yes God they're wicked, kill them all.*" He STOOD representing the heart of God, reflecting God's heart back to him, while petitioning for souls to be saved rather than being destroyed. As we study this passage of scripture, we discern that Abraham continued to peradventure God until he interceded for ten people to be saved.

Abraham STOOD in sonship and governed over his bloodline, the land of Solomon, the people, and the region. He was able to save a few even as God had planned to judge all the same.

What is your heart posture as God reveals his plans to you?

- Do you have a heart for people or even care about their souls?
- Do you care about the eternal state of people?
- Do you have or desire the grace and mercy of God to be considered when judgement has risen?
- Do you even know that you can petition God for intel and stand interceding based on what he says?

I am posing these questions because I am witnessing so many people having dreams, visions, enlightenments, mysteries, and prophetic intel, but they share them with no kingdom governance.

- They do not have any proceeding revelation or guidance as to what to do with what they are sharing.
- They have no heart, grace, or mercy for the people, lands, regions, and nations being exposed, judged, and destroyed.

- They do not intercede for mercy and are often giving their self-righteous prideful reasons for why people, lands, regions, and nations deserve the judgement or calamity that is coming to them.

- They have no regard for loved ones and righteous ones that are impacted.

- Others who have received similar intel tend to join with these people and further strengthen their posture for seeing exposure, scandal, judgments, and calamity unfolding. There is no unction to unite in intercession or a righteous agenda that is about reconciliation, restoration, or soul winning.

- The main focus tends to be waiting on the word to ensue so they can prove they heard from the Lord – prove the accuracy of their intel.

- When it comes to exposure, people tend to also add their own perception to whatever insights they receive. They entertain the tickling ears of others who are more into gossip, strife, scandal, demise of others. There is no regard for word curses and fiery darts being released as people gossip and get on the band wagon to speak their suspicions, intuitions, opinions, inquiries, confirmations.

  2Timothy 4:3-4 *For the time will come when they will not endure sound doctrine; but after their own lusts shall they heap to themselves teachers, having itching ears; And they shall turn away their ears from the truth, and shall be turned unto fables. But watch thou in all things, endure afflictions, do the work of an evangelist, make full proof of thy ministry.*

  There is also no consideration for loved ones or for exploration of whether restoration is possible for the person. These people try to make their heartlessness be biblical. But really, many of them are immature, prideful, callous, malicious, vindictive, have unresolved trauma, are bitter and validated by their gifts and callings, and they lack the character and nature of God. We hear their issues in their words, but we disregard their fruit. Our ears lustfully itch for the entertainment of their fables. Jonah operated in this manner and ended up in the belly of a fish.

From Dr. Taquetta Bakers Book, "Fivefold Operations Volume I."

When studying the book of Jonah, we find God giving Jonah an assignment to go cry aloud against the wickedness of the people of Nineveh. Jonah, instead, paid a fare to flee to Tarnish by way of a ship because he did not want to give the word. His reason being he knew that if they repented, God would deliver them. Jonah was on the ship sleeping while the men were seeking God for the purpose of the tumultuous judging winds that seemed to roar as they were sailing to Tarnish. The shipmaster woke Jonah up and demanded he cry out to God with them. After casting lots and Jonah confessing, it was revealed that the evil winds were due to him running from God. They had no choice but to throw him overboard to get the evil winds to cease. Once overboard a fish swallowed Jonah. He was inside the fish for three days and three nights, and reluctantly humbled himself while there. God spared him, the fish vomited Jonah on dry land, and God required him again to go deliver his word to Nineveh.

In Jonah chapter 3, Jonah released the word God gave him for Nineveh. They were pricked to conviction by Jonah's outcry, and sought God with fasting and repentance. God accepted their fast and repentance and withdrew his judgment.

Verse 5-10 *So the people of Nineveh believed God, and proclaimed a fast, and put on sackcloth, from the greatest of them even to the least of them. For word came unto the king of Nineveh, and he arose from his throne, and he laid his robe from him, and covered him with sackcloth, and sat in ashes. And he caused it to be proclaimed and published through Nineveh by the decree of the king and his nobles, saying, Let neither man nor beast, herd nor flock, taste any thing: let them not feed, nor drink water: But let man and beast be covered with sackcloth, and cry mightily unto God: yea, let them turn every one from his evil way, and from the violence that is in their hands. Who can tell if God will turn and repent, and turn away from his fierce anger, that we perish not? And God saw their works, that they turned from their evil way; and God repented of the evil, that he had said that he would do unto them; and he did it not.*

Jonah was displeased by God's forgiveness. He was so grieved by it and thus wanted to die. He told God that the reason he fled from proclaiming the word was because he knew God would forgive them and withdraw his judgement.

Jonah 4:1-3 *But it displeased Jonah exceedingly, and he was very angry. And he prayed unto the Lord, and said, I pray thee, O Lord, was not this my saying, when I was yet in my country? Therefore I fled before unto Tarshish: for I knew that thou art a gracious God, and merciful, slow to anger, and of great kindness, and repentest thee of the evil. Therefore now, O Lord, take, I beseech thee, my life from me; for it is better for me to die than to live.*

What a horrible posture for a saint but especially a mouthpiece of God. Fleeing so he would not have to give a word that would turn a people back to God, then being grieved unto death that restoration occurred. As Jonah grieved, God took him through a trial to show him that his posture as a prophet was ungodly. Even in that trial, Jonah was self-absorbed and asked God to kill him, so he did not have to endure the trial. He was not able to recognize that God was using the situation to prove a point of how repentance and restoration rather than death and destruction was his ultimate desire with his people.

Verse 4-11 *Then said the Lord, Doest thou well to be angry? So Jonah went out of the city, and sat on the east side of the city, and there made him a* *booth, and sat under it in the shadow, till he might see what would become of the city. And the Lord God prepared a gourd, and made it to come up over Jonah, that it might be a shadow over his head, to deliver him from his grief. So Jonah was exceeding glad of the gourd. But God prepared a worm when the morning rose the next day, and it smote the gourd that it withered. And it came to pass, when the sun did arise, that God prepared a vehement east wind; and the sun beat upon the head of Jonah, that he fainted, and wished in himself to die, and said, It is better for me to die than to live. And God said to Jonah, Doest thou well to be angry for the gourd? And he said, I do well to be angry, even unto death. Then said the Lord, Thou hast had pity on the gourd, for the which thou hast not laboured, neither madest it grow; which came up in a night, and perished in a night: And should not I spare Nineveh, that great city, wherein are more than sixscore thousand persons that cannot discern between their right hand and their left hand; and also much cattle?*

Ezekiel 3:18 *If I say to the wicked, 'You shall surely die,' and you give him no warning, nor speak to warn the wicked from his wicked way, in order to save his life, that wicked person shall die for his iniquity, but his blood I will require at your hand.*

Prophets with Jonah's disposition are dangerous. They have the gift, office, and authority of God but not the character, nature, and heart of God.

- They would rather see people judged, suffering, and destroyed than restored in right fellowship with God.
- They are vexed when God forgives because they want to see the warnings and judgments come to pass.
- They try to usurp God by striving to punish the people for their sins rather than allowing the word to be the punishment needed to drive people to repentance and right fellowship with God.
- They either do not discern or dread that God's prophecies, even his warnings, cautions, corrections, and judgments are not about harming people, but about provoking people to deliverance.

Such prophets will go to great lengths to have their judgments manifest, even to the extent of refusing to give warnings, and risking their own relationships and lives being destroyed. This is not God's posture for a prophet. God's prophet has his heart. God so loved the world that he gave his only begotten son that we should not perish but have everlasting life (***John 3:16***). This is the heart of a

prophet – that he or she would sacrifice their own lives so that others might be saved. Jesus just wanted to please God. This was his meat and his will, even at the expense of his own life.
John 4:34 *Jesus saith unto them, My meat is to do the will of him that sent me, and to finish his work.*

Another way heartless prophets operate, is by giving warnings, cautions, corrections, and judgments that God did not release. It will be for the purpose of getting people to repent for matters the prophet believes the people should turn from or should do. Often such words are given by an immature or wounded prophet who has not been taught how to properly govern in the office of a prophet and who is not grounded in the character and nature of the Lord. Though not always the case,

- They may contend they are called to warn and judge.

- They may be adamant that this is their calling, while lacking understanding and balance in the full official duties of a prophet.

- Their prophets' blessings and exhortations are usually soulish, conditional, and self-serving. They are to draw people to them and ensue favor with people than to draw them to God. The minute a person does

> something they do not like, they become offended, or their word is rejected, they withdraw their blessings and exhortations and release false warnings and damnations.

I would contend that the only time there should be a scoffing at the demise of a person, place, or thing, is when God is requiring it, and even then, it should be at his leading and guidance, and should be revealed that he is requiring it. As even the passage below God reveals, that he will mock those who he is exposing and judging, it is not stating that we the conduits of his intel should do it.

Proverbs 1:1-6 *The proverbs of Solomon the son of David, king of Israel. To know wisdom and instruction; to perceive the words of understanding; To receive the instruction of wisdom, justice, and judgment, and equity; To give subtilty to the simple, to the young man knowledge and discretion. A wise man will hear, and will increase learning; and a man of understanding shall attain unto wise counsels: To understand a proverb, and the interpretation; the words of the wise, and their dark sayings.*

Proverbs 1:7-11 *The fear of the LORD is the beginning of knowledge: but fools despise wisdom and instruction. My son, hear the instruction of thy father, and forsake not the law of thy mother: For they shall be an ornament of grace unto thy head, and chains about thy neck. My son, if sinners entice thee, consent thou not.*

Proverbs 1:20-33 *Wisdom crieth without; she uttereth her voice in the streets: She crieth in the chief place of* *concourse, in the openings of the gates: in the city she uttereth her words, saying, How long, ye simple ones, will ye love simplicity? and the scorners in their scorning, and fools hate knowledge? Turn you at my reproof: behold, I will pour out my spirit unto you, I will make known my words unto you. Because I have called, and ye refused; I have stretched out my hand, and no man regarded; But ye have set at nought all my counsel, and would none of my reproof:*

I also will laugh at your calamity; I will mock when your fear cometh; When your fear cometh as desolation, and your destruction cometh as a whirlwind; when distress and anguish cometh upon you. Then shall they call upon me, but I will not answer; they shall seek me early, but they shall not find me: For that they hated knowledge, and did not choose the fear of the LORD: They would none of my counsel: they despised all my reproof. Therefore shall they eat of the fruit of their own way, and be filled with their own devices. For the turning away of the simple shall slay them, and the prosperity of fools shall destroy them. But whoso hearkeneth unto me shall dwell safely, and shall be quiet from fear of evil.

The scoffing and mocking should feel and be clear that it is coming from God himself and not you personally. We experience this with the Old Testament prophets. When they released prophetic words that included rebuke, correction, chastisement, warning, judgement, exposure, mockery, scoffing, laughing at the calamity of a person, place, or thing, it was clear that this was ALL from GOD and was the posture of GOD. Their flesh, perceptions, emotions, carnalities, and lustful desires were not intertwined, perceived, or glorified in the prophecy.

- ✓ We do not find them returning to boast or defend the intel they released from a personal standpoint or speaking, responding, or gloating personally on the demise of a person, place, or thing.
- ✓ We do not find them operating unseemingly where people were more focused on them and their actions than the intel God was releasing.
- ✓ If and when they do defend, it is at the leading of God or further revelation on the intel at hand.

I pray we are discerning truth of the character and nature of the Old Testament prophets. Please take time to study them and their prophetic utterances and insights. Examine their heart posture with God and how they died to self to be pure conduits and embodiments of God's word.

APOSTOLIC WATCH PROPHECY TO ENDTIME SCOUTS

Prophetic Intel for 2024 and beyond – Apostolic Watch January 7, 2024: Apostle Taquetta Baker

Please study and ask God for intel on the book of Revelation. Let it play at night as you sleep and during the day in your atmosphere. Do not worry about whether you understand it or not. Trust God to download clarity and intel to you as you embody the chapters of Revelation.

The demonic sounds, even of creatures that you hear in this hour are ancient principalities that have been dormant in demonic kingdoms. They are now resurfacing, while gathering and positioning themselves in regions and spheres for end time attack. This is the reason I keep fervently encouraging my people to get on the walls of intercession, SHIFT into unwavering faith, take their sonship seat as storehouse agents, and SHIFT at spiritual gates to govern regions, nations, and spheres in subduing dominion says the Lord.

Psalm 24 *The earth is the LORD's, and the fulness thereof; the world, and they that dwell therein. For he hath founded it upon the seas, and established it upon the floods. Who shall ascend into the hill of the LORD? or who shall stand in his holy place? He that hath clean hands, and a pure heart; who hath not lifted up his soul unto vanity, nor sworn deceitfully. He shall receive the blessing from the LORD, and righteousness from the God of his salvation. This is the generation of them that seek him, that seek thy face, O Jacob. Selah. Lift up your heads, O ye gates; and be ye lift up, ye everlasting doors; and the King of glory shall come in. Who is this King of glory? The LORD strong and mighty, the LORD mighty in battle. Lift up your heads, O ye gates; even lift them up, ye everlasting doors; and the King of glory shall come in. Who is this King of glory? The LORD of hosts, he is the King of glory. Selah.*

Isaiah 2:4 *And he shall judge among the nations, and shall rebuke many people: and they shall beat their swords into plowshares, and their spears into pruninghooks: nation shall not lift up sword against nation, neither shall they learn war any more.*

Micah 4:3-7 *And he shall judge among many people, and rebuke strong nations afar off; and they shall beat their swords into plowshares, and their spears into pruninghooks: nation shall not lift up a sword against nation, neither shall they learn war any more. But they* *shall sit every man under his vine and under his fig tree; and none shall make them afraid: for the mouth of the LORD of hosts hath spoken it. For all people will walk every one in the name of his god, and we will walk in the name of the LORD our God for ever and ever. In that day, saith the LORD, will I assemble her that halteth, and I will gather her that is driven out, and her that I have afflicted; And I will make her that halted a remnant, and her that was cast far off a strong nation: and the LORD shall reign over them in mount Zion from henceforth, even for ever.*

Psalm 2:7-12 *I will declare the decree: the LORD hath said unto me, Thou art my Son; this day have I begotten thee. Ask of me, and I shall give thee the heathen for thine inheritance, and the uttermost parts of the earth for thy possession. Thou shalt break them with a rod of iron; thou shalt dash them in pieces like a potter's vessel. Be wise now therefore, O ye kings: be instructed, ye judges of the earth. Serve the LORD with fear, and rejoice with trembling. Kiss the Son, lest he be angry, and ye perish from the way, when his wrath is kindled but a little. Blessed are all they that put their trust in him.*

Revelations 2:26-29 *And he that overcometh, and keepeth my works unto the end, to him will I give power over the nations: And he shall rule them with a rod of iron; as the vessels of a potter shall they be broken to shivers: even as I received of my Father. And I will give him the morning star. He that hath an ear, let him hear what the Spirit saith unto the churches.*

Revelations 19:11-16 *And I saw heaven opened, and behold a white horse; and he that sat upon him was called Faithful and True, and in righteousness he doth judge and make war. -- His eyes were as a flame of fire, and on his head were many crowns; and he had a name written, that no man knew, but he himself. And he was clothed with a vesture dipped in blood: and his name is called The Word of God. And the armies which were in heaven followed him upon white horses, clothed in fine linen, white and clean. And out of his mouth goeth a sharp sword, that with it he should smite the nations: and he shall rule them with a rod of iron: and he treadeth the winepress of the fierceness and wrath of Almighty God. And he hath on his vesture and on his thigh a name written, KING OF KINGS, AND LORD OF LORDS.*

- ✓ *Govern atmospherically, says the Lord.*

- ✓ *Govern the sound waves, weather patterns, frequency, and airwaves in spiritual and natural realms.*

- ✓ *Govern in the full dominion in supernatural realms and regions and not just in earthly spheres of what you see and experience.*

- ✓ *Clearly legislate what is being released, the sounds, the culture trends, the fear mongering, the demonic sounds of ancient principalities, demonic systems, and demonic kingdoms. Overthrow them with my voice, my revelations, my truths, my principles, my scriptural revelations, my intel, heavenly sounds – spiritual songs, prophetic songs and utterances, declarative and demonstrative sounds, instrumental sounds, kingdom keys and melodies from heaven, says the Lord.*

TAKE UP RESIDENCE IN THE ATMOSPHERE AND SPIRITUAL REALMS BY LEGISLATING THE KINGDOM OF HEAVEN IN YOUR SPHERE.

Matthew 6:9-13 *After this manner therefore pray ye: Our Father which art in heaven, Hallowed be thy name. Thy kingdom come. Thy will be done in earth, as it is in heaven. Give us this day our daily bread.*

Revelation 11:15 *Then the seventh angel sounded: And there were loud voices in heaven, saying, "The kingdoms of this world have become the kingdoms of our Lord and of His Christ, and He shall reign forever and ever!"*

Ephesians 2:6 *contends that we are seated in heavenly places in Christ Jesus. And hath raised us up together, and made us sit together in heavenly places in Christ Jesus. And hath raised us up together and made us sit together in heavenly places in Christ Jesus.*

The Amplified Bible *And He raised us up together with Him and made us sit down together [giving us joint seating with Him] in the heavenly sphere [by virtue of our being] in Christ Jesus (the Messiah, the Anointed One).*

Set is *sygkathizō* in Greek and means:

1. to give (or take) a seat in company with
2. (make) sit (down) together.
3. to cause to sit down together, place together
4. to sit down together

Dictionary.com defines *set* as:

1. to put (something or someone) in a particular place
2. to place in a particular position or posture
3. to place in some relation to something or someone
4. to put into some condition
5. to put or apply
6. to put in the proper position
7. to put in the proper or desired order or condition for use
8. to post, station, or appoint for the purpose of performing some duty

Heavenly places are heavenly regions. They are the supernatural realms and dimensions that we refer to and must recondition our mind to live in and from.

Since this is the finished work after the cross, the word *set* denotes an eternal place - an eternal authority and governing in God - an established seat of authority inside the heavenly realms in Christ.

Through your established seat, you commune with Jesus Christ as he delivers, heals, and transforms you into Christlikeness.

2Corinthians 3:18 *But we all, with open face beholding as in a glass the glory of the Lord, are changed into the same image from glory to glory, even as by the Spirit of the Lord.*

New Living Bible *So all of us who have had that veil removed can see and reflect the glory of the Lord. And the Lord—who is the Spirit—makes us more and more like him as we are changed into his glorious image.*

As we mature in Christ likeness, Jesus Christ reveals the mysteries and realities of the kingdom of heaven to you such that your seat expands, and he allows you to be privy to heavenly visions, wisdom, revelation, knowledge, counsel, might, judgements, justice, translations, the literal kingdom of heaven, storehouses, weaponry, and provision.

We must have clarity that we are eternal beings - we are not of the earthly world. From the beginning, we were meant to live from a posture of eternal dominion.

Genesis 1:28 *And God blessed them, and God said unto them, Be fruitful, and multiply, and replenish the earth, and subdue it: and have dominion over the fish of the sea, and over the fowl of the air, and over every living thing that moveth upon the earth.*

Psalm 8:4-6 *What is man, that thou art mindful of him? and the son of man, that thou visitest him? For thou hast made him a little lower than the angels, and hast crowned him with glory and honour. Thou madest him to have* *dominion over the works of thy hands; thou hast put all things under his feet.*

Philippians 3:20 *But our citizenship is in heaven, and we eagerly await a Savior from there, the Lord Jesus Christ.*

James 4:4 *You adulterous people! Do you not know that friendship with the world is enmity with God? Therefore whoever wishes to be a friend of the world makes himself an enemy of God.*

Dominion denotes a kingdom throne of reigning, ruling, governing, and prevailing in the spirit and authority of God. Jesus came to restore the dominion that crumbled through the fall of man. Even as Jesus Christ walked the earth as a natural man, he made it clear that he was not of this world, and we were not of this world. He maintained a heavenly perspective and was a demonstrator of dominion - of how we should live daily from this truth.

John 17:14-19 *I have given them your word. And the world hates them because they do not belong to the world, just as I do not belong to the world. I'm not asking you to take them out of the world, but to keep them safe from the evil one. They do not belong to this world any more than I do. Make them holy by your truth; teach them your word, which is truth. Just as you sent me into the world, I am sending them into the world. And I give myself as a holy sacrifice for them so they can be made holy by your truth.*

Without a dominion posture and perspective, you will be inconsistent with living and governing from a heavenly perspective. You may have a mind to rule but will conduct your rulership from the earth and the second heaven.

Ephesians 1:15-23 *Wherefore I also, after I heard of your faith in the Lord Jesus, and love unto all the saints, Cease not to give thanks for you, making mention of you in my prayers; That the God of our Lord Jesus Christ, the Father of glory, may give unto you the spirit of wisdom and revelation in the knowledge of him: The eyes of your understanding being enlightened; that ye may know what is the hope of his calling, and what the riches of the glory of his inheritance in the saints, And what is the exceeding greatness of his power to us-ward who believe, according to the working of his mighty power, Which he wrought in Christ, when he raised him from the dead, and set him at his own right hand in the heavenly places, Far above all principality, and power, and might, and dominion, and every name that is named, not only in this world, but also in that which is to come: And hath put all things under his feet, and gave him to be the head over all things to the church, Which is his body, the fulness of him that filleth all in all.*

Whoever owns the atmosphere, sea, the region, and the land will rule and govern, says the Lord. God is wanting his people, especially fivefold officers, intercessory scouts, and seers, to govern and take up jurisdiction in regions and spheres. Do not just pray but govern – claim your people, lands, regions, spheres of influence, and atmospheres by gatekeeping and owning the inheritance I have given you through them. Push back principalities, powers, rulers of darkness, and territorial spirits, while commanding my kingdom to take up residence in your midst. Partner with the angels, courts of heaven, and other believers to gatekeep in dominion for my glory. Nullify Baal worship, Mammon, anti-Christ agendas, anti-gender agendas, anti-restitution agendas especially with African and Native-American ethnicities, and combat ancient principalities coming up from demonic kingdoms that are gathering to war in these end times.

Revelation 20:7-10 *And when the thousand years are expired, Satan shall be loosed out of his prison, And shall go out to deceive the nations which are in the four quarters of the earth, Gog and Magog, to gather them together to battle: the number of whom is as the sand of the sea. And they went up on the breadth of the earth, and compassed the camp of the saints about, and the beloved city: and fire came down from God out of heaven, and devoured them. And the devil that deceived them was cast into the lake of fire and brimstone, where the beast and the false prophet are, and shall be tormented day and night for ever and ever.*

Revelation 20:11-21 *And I saw heaven opened, and behold a white horse; and he that sat upon him was called Faithful and True, and in righteousness he doth judge and make war. -- His eyes were as a flame of fire, and on his head were many crowns; and he had a name written, that no man knew, but he himself. And he was clothed with a* *vesture dipped in blood: and his name is called The Word of God. And the armies which were in heaven followed him upon white horses, clothed in fine linen, white and clean. And out of his mouth goeth a sharp sword, that with it he should smite the nations: and he shall rule them with a rod of iron: and he treadeth the winepress of the fierceness and wrath of Almighty God. And he hath on his vesture and on his thigh a name written, KING OF KINGS, AND LORD OF LORDS.*

And I saw an angel standing in the sun; and he cried with a loud voice, saying to all the fowls that fly in the midst of heaven, Come and gather yourselves together unto the supper of the great God; That ye may eat the flesh of kings, and the flesh of captains, and the flesh of mighty men, and the flesh of horses, and of them that sit on them, and the flesh of all men, both free and bond, both small and great.

And I saw the beast, and the kings of the earth, and their armies, gathered together to make war against him that sat on the horse, and against his army. And the beast was taken, and with him the false prophet that wrought miracles before him, with which he deceived them that had received the mark of the beast, and them that worshipped his image. These both were cast alive into a lake of fire burning with brimstone. And the remnant were slain with the sword of him that sat upon the horse, which sword proceeded out of his mouth: and all the fowls were filled with their flesh.

This description of a scout is from my manual, "Unmasking The Powers Of A Scout Volume I."

When you are called as an intercessory watchman for a person, ministry, business, organization, or region, you are serving in the position of a scout.

A scout operates in the offensive positions of a watchman, seer, prophet, dreamer, intercessor, soldier, stealth bomber, and sniper. Scouts are employed to inspect, observe, or survey the enemy in order to gain and gather information for military purposes. You observe and report on the following:

- Their character, nature, and personality,
- Abilities and capabilities,
- Likes and dislikes,
- Habits and patterns,
- Strengths and weaknesses,
- Movements, locations, and operations,
- Strategies and techniques,
- Environments and habitats to which they maneuver and dwell,
- Their identity, purpose, and mission,
- Their personal, geographical, and generational power and operation,
- History, culture, language, and communication strategies.

Your intel is beneficial to being offensive against the enemy, while annihilating any present or future plan of attack or counterattack.

A scout is the eyes and ears for the army of the Lord. When intel is needed on the enemy, you can maneuver around the enemy's camp or on the battle ground and collect intel.

Scouts this is your hour of SHINNING. Your keen eyes and scouting ventures are needed in this hour. I need you to be the balance between the horrid mess from the unbelieving and carnal lukewarm tickling of the saints ears and the truth bearers that will be at war in this hour and seasons to come. I need you to be the balance in discerning and sounding the alarm on where and who the war really is with as I download and give you keen intel on dreams, visions, translations, and spiritual warfare prayers.

Sound the alarm that this is not a flesh and blood fight.

Sound the alarm as I reveal to you the true enemy of that moment, and in this hour, and how to combat and overthrow it.

Sound the alarm as you remain in my abiding peace, and not allow your righteous indignation to cause you to attack people or even focus on demons that are not the true root or stronghold of the issue. Sound the alarm as I reveal to you the true enemy, the true adversary that is working in this hour to steal, kill, and destroy my godly agenda, the fruit and harvest of my labors and in order to have people distracted while the enemy unveils his true agenda for such a time as this.

For indeed this is a season of exposure, but the division and bleeding trauma that you see in the natural has a greater agenda in the spirit. Do not get caught up in the hype, launch out into the deep for spiritual mysteries, and intel that will manifest change, heal the broken hearted, and set captives free. For this is who you are my Kingdom seer agents that scout out the land and overthrow darkness for my glory.

This year I am calling you out of the shadows forward. Do not worry about who receives you or rejects you. Take your place with confidence and trust that I have created and yielded this space for you. As you are obedient to me, I will use you to expose true enemies. Those that once ostracized you and that may even question your motives in this present season, will flock to you as you stand trusting me to use you for my glory.

Stay Focused

Colossians 2:6-10 The Amplifier Bible *Therefore as you have received Christ Jesus the Lord, walk in [union with] Him [reflecting His character in the things you do and say—living lives that lead others away from sin], having been deeply rooted [in Him] and now being continually built up in Him and [becoming increasingly more] established in your faith, just as you were taught, and overflowing in it with gratitude. See to it that no one takes you captive through philosophy and empty deception [pseudo-intellectual babble], according to the* *tradition [and musings] of mere men, following the elementary principles of this world, rather than following [the truth—the teachings of] Christ. For in Him all the fullness of Deity (the Godhead) dwells in bodily form [completely expressing the divine essence of God]. And in Him you have been made complete [achieving spiritual stature through Christ], and He is the head over all rule and authority [of every angelic and earthly power].*

The Message Bible *My counsel for you is simple and straightforward: Just go ahead with what you've been given. You received Christ Jesus, the Master; now live him. You're deeply rooted in him. You're well constructed upon him. You know your way around the faith. Now do what you've been taught. School's out; quit studying the subject and start living it! And let your living spill over into thanksgiving. Watch out for people who try to dazzle you with big words and intellectual double-talk. They want to drag you off into endless arguments that never amount to anything. They spread their ideas through the empty traditions of human beings and the empty superstitions of spirit beings. But that's not the way of Christ. Everything of God gets expressed in him, so you can see and hear him clearly. You don't need a telescope, a microscope, or a horoscope to realize the fullness of Christ, and the emptiness of the universe without him. When you come to him, that fullness comes* *together for you, too. His power extends over everything.*

Possess Relentless Faith

1Corinthians 15:58 *Therefore, my dear brothers, stand firm. Let nothing move you. Always give yourselves fully to the work of the Lord, because you know that your labor in the Lord is not in vain.*

Operate in Keenness

- Finely sharpened, as an edge; so shaped as to cut or pierce substances readily
- Characterized by strength and distinctness of perception; extremely sensitive or responsive
- Having or showing great mental penetration or acumen (keen insight or shrewdness)

Matthew 10:16 *Behold, I send you forth as sheep in the midst of wolves: be ye therefore wise as serpents, and harmless as doves.*

The Amplified Bible *Listen carefully: I am sending you out like sheep among wolves; so be wise as serpents (cunning, clever, sly), and innocent as doves [have no self-serving agenda].*

The Message Bible *Stay alert. This is hazardous work I'm assigning you. You're going to be like sheep running through a wolf pack, so don't call attention to yourselves. Be as shrewd as a snake, inoffensive as a dove.*

Be Holy & Blameless

1Peter 1:16 *Because it is written, Be ye holy; for I am holy.*

Leviticus 11:44 *For I am the Lord your God: ye shall therefore sanctify yourselves, and ye shall be holy; for I am holy: neither shall ye defile yourselves with any manner of creeping thing that creepeth upon the earth.*

Hebrews 12:14 *Make every effort to live in peace with everyone and to be holy; without holiness no one will see the Lord.*

Hebrews 7:26 *Such a high priest truly meets our need—one who is holy, blameless, pure, set apart from sinners, exalted above the heavens.*

1Corinthians 1:2 *To the church of God in Corinth, to those sanctified in Christ Jesus and called to be his holy people, together with all those everywhere who call on the name of our Lord Jesus Christ—their Lord and ours.*

Holy means to be:

1. viewed as a saint of God
2. be set apart
3. deemed sacred (physically, pure, morally blameless or religious, ceremonially, consecrated)

Colossians 1:22 *In the body of his flesh through death, to present you holy and unblameable and unreproveable in his sight.*

Unblameable is *amōmos* in Greek and means:

1. unblemished (literally or figuratively)
2. without blame (blemish, fault, spot), faultless, unblamable.
3. without rebuke, without blame, without spot, without fault
4. without blemish, as a sacrifice without spot or blemish
5. morally: without blemish, faultless, unblameable

Unreprovable is *anegklētos* in Greek and means:

1. unaccused, i.e. (by implication) irreproachable, innocent
2. that cannot be called into to account, unable to corrupt, unreproveable, unaccused, blameless

- Oxford dictionary defines blameless as innocent of wrongdoing.

Jude 1:24 *Now to him who is able to keep you from stumbling and to present blameless before the presence of his glory with great joy,*

Ephesians 5:27-28 *That he might present it to himself a glorious church, not having spot, or wrinkle, or any such thing; but that it should be holy and without blemish. So that he might present the church to himself in splendor, without spot or wrinkle or any such thing, that she might be holy and without blemish.*
Endeavoring to live holy and blameless is vital to not:

- Causing reproach upon God and his kingdom.
- Presenting mixture, carnality, and worldliness with godly intel, such that people reject him, his warnings, judgments, rebukes, and insights.
- Succumbing to gossip, slander, ridicule, judgment, and being a castaway.
  1Corinthians 9:27 *But I keep under my body, and bring it into subjection: lest that by any means, when I have preached to others, I myself should be a castaway.*

Be Obedient

Proverbs 13:13 *He who scorns instruction will pay for it, but he who respects a command is rewarded.*

Proverbs 16:20 *Whoever gives heed to instruction prospers, and blessed is he who trusts in the Lord.*

Proverbs 19:16 *He who obeys instructions guards his life, but he who is contemptuous of his ways will die.*

John 14:15 *If you love me, you will keep my commandments.*

1Peter 1:14 *As obedient children, do not be conformed to the passions of your former ignorance.*

Acts 5:29 *But Peter and the apostles answered, "We must obey God rather than men."*

1John 5:3 *For this is the love of God, that we keep his commandments. And his commandments are not burdensome.*

Isaiah 1:19 *If you are willing and obedient, you shall eat the good of the land.*

1Samuel 15:22 *And Samuel said, Hath the LORD as great delight in burnt offerings and sacrifices, As in obeying the voice of the LORD? Behold, to obey is better than sacrifice, And to hearken than the fat of rams. For rebellion is as the sin of witchcraft, And stubbornness is as iniquity and idolatry.*

Be Confident

Hebrews 10:35-36 *Do not, therefore, fling away your [fearless] confidence, for it has a glorious and great reward. For you have need of patient endurance [to bear up under difficult circumstances without compromising], so that when you have carried out the will of God, you may receive and enjoy to the full what is promised.*

Philippians 1:6 *Being confident of this, that he who began a good work in you will carry it on to completion until the day of Christ Jesus.*

Joshua 1:9 The Amplified Bible *Have I not commanded you? Be strong and courageous! Do not be terrified or dismayed (intimidated), for the LORD your God is with you wherever you go.*

Be Fervent & Steadfast

Romans 12:10-11 *Be devoted to one another in brotherly love; give preference to one another in honor, not lagging in diligence, fervent in spirit, serving the Lord.*

The Message Bible *Love from the center of who you are; don't fake it. Run for dear life from evil; hold on for dear life to good. Be good friends who love deeply; practice playing second fiddle. Don't burn out; keep yourselves fueled and aflame. Be* *alert servants of the Master, cheerfully expectant. Don't quit in hard times; pray all the harder. Help needy Christians; be inventive in hospitality.*

PURSUING GODLY WISDOM FOR GOVERNING INTEL

Seeking God For Intel

Intel includes dreams, visions, enlightenments, mysteries, prophecies, words of revelation and knowledge especially those that present as rebukes, reproof, chastisements, exposure, warnings, judgments, calamities, etc.

Sometimes, I have a knowing of a matter. Holy Spirit will just impress within me to know a matter by the knowledge and truth of God.

Ephesians 1:18 *The eyes of your understanding being enlightened; that ye may know what is the hope of his calling, and what the riches of the glory of his inheritance in the saints.*

Matthew 13:11 *He answered and said unto them, Because it is given unto you to know the mysteries of the kingdom of heaven, but to them it is not given.*

Luke 8:10 *He replied, "The knowledge of the mysteries of the kingdom of God has been given to you, but to others I speak in parables, so that, 'Though seeing, they may not see; though hearing, they may not understand.'*

- Pray into the intel for a proceeding revelation, insight, and strategies. Keeping seeking God and bringing that dream, vision, prophecy, revelation, back before God until he speaks or until you are clear in your spirit that there is no proceeding intel. Sometimes, God wants to build you in pursuing him and abiding in his presence. He wants to teach you how to rely on him and stay the course in pursuing his voice and mysteries. We claim to love God and his presence, but we dread abiding and pursuing the deeper things of God. We dread having to govern over the covenant relationship we have with him and being accountable and active in resting, living, and engaging him and in his presence.

  We perceive God not immediately speaking as rejection or we become frustrated and pursue other people or other methods of interpreting, clarifying, or providing proceeding intel on our revelation. This is okay sometimes, and for baby believers. But it is not okay for mature believers who should truly know how to abide and strive with God. Those who understand who they are as SONS and can STAND before God like Abraham did.

Abraham kept inquiring with God. He did not take God not completely relinquishing the judgment as rejection. He did not take having to constantly intercede for greater mercy as rejection. He allowed the dominion rights of his sonship to legislate for him. Habakkuk, Isaiah, and Jesus Christ, encouraged continual supplication of prayer with God.

Habbukak 2:1-3 *I will stand upon my watch, and set me upon the tower, and will watch to see what he will say unto me, and what I shall answer when I am reproved. And the LORD answered me, and said, Write the vision, and make it plain upon tables, that he may run that readeth it. For the vision is yet for an appointed time, but at the end it shall speak, and not lie: though it tarry, wait for it; because it will surely come, it will not tarry.*

Isaiah 49:16 *Behold, I have inscribed you on the palms of My hands; your walls are ever before Me.*

Isaiah 62:6-7 *On your walls, Jerusalem, I have appointed watchmen; All day and all night they will never keep silent. You who profess the LORD, take no rest for yourselves; And give Him no rest until He establishes and makes Jerusalem an object of praise on the earth.*

Luke 18:1 *Then Jesus told them a parable about their need to pray at all times and not lose heart.*

- Preadventure for grace, mercy, and a lesser judgment.

- Keep standing and preadventuring until you are clear that you have received God's final disposition on the matter.

- Admonish God to see if he would change a judgment based on the favor you have with him, as sometimes God will change his mind because of his love for you.

- If God follows through with a judgment, seek him for intel on how to protect and save yourself, your loved ones, the innocent, and righteous. Do what God says even if it seems simple or as if it would not have a natural power. Remember God's ways, strategies, methods, and weaponry are not like ours. God uses the foolish things to confound the wise (***1Corinthians 1:27-31***).

- Seek God for his heart and character posture as he releases intel through you. Endeavor to represent him while dying to self. Decrease so that God can increase and get **ALL** the glory from how he is using you (***John 3:30-35***).

- Allow God to defend you and his intel. If you are challenged regarding how you are being persecuted, rejected, dishonored, and afflicted, share your thoughts and feelings with God or a mentor, spiritual parent, or leader. Do not bleed on the people or God's word. Do not SHIFT into acts that cause you to operate unseemingly or become blameful and reproachable before the people. When the people persecuted and rejected Jesus Christ, they did it out of their own will, not because they found anything regarding Satan, sin, or their evil acts in him. This is what it means to be blameless and unreproachable.

John 4:30 *Hereafter I will not talk much with you: for the prince of this world cometh, and hath nothing in me.*

John 15:1-11 *I am the true vine, and my Father is the husbandman. Every branch in me that beareth not fruit he taketh away: and every branch that beareth fruit, he purgeth it, that it may bring forth more fruit. Now ye are clean through the word which I have spoken unto you. Abide in me, and I in you. As the branch cannot bear fruit of itself, except it abide in the vine; no more can ye, except ye abide in me. I am the vine, ye are the branches: He that abideth in me, and I in him, the same bringeth forth much fruit: for without me ye can do nothing. If a man abide not in me, he is cast forth as a branch, and is withered; and men gather them, and cast them into the fire, and they are burned.*

If ye abide in me, and my words abide in you, ye shall ask what ye will, and it shall be done unto you. Herein is my Father glorified, that ye bear much fruit; so shall ye be my disciples. As the Father hath loved me, so have I loved you: continue ye in my love. If ye keep my commandments, ye shall abide in my love; even as I have kept my Father's commandments, and abide in his love. These things have I spoken unto you, that my joy might remain in you, and that your joy might be full.

Heart posture, fruit, and motive is everything, as it determines what well and authority we are speaking from. Persecution, rejection, and affliction does not give us a pass for bleeding on those we are to release God's word to.

Acts 20:22-27 *And now, behold, I go bound in the spirit unto Jerusalem, not knowing the things that shall befall me there: Save that the Holy Ghost witnesseth in every city, saying that bonds and afflictions abide me. But none of these things move me, neither count I my life dear unto myself, so that I might finish my course with joy, and the ministry, which I have received of the Lord Jesus, to testify the gospel of the grace of God. And now, behold, I know that ye all, among whom I have gone preaching the kingdom of God, shall see my face no more. Wherefore I take you to record this day, that I am pure from the blood of all men. For I have not shunned to declare unto you all the counsel of God.*

We always want to make sure we are speaking from the well and authority of God and his Holy Spirit that guides, leads, and embodies us. God is moved by our infirmities just like he was with Jesus Christ in the garden of Getheseme. We should be expressing our traumas regarding the impact of being intel carriers to him, not beating up those he has us speaking to.

Hebrews 4:15-16 *For we have not an high priest which cannot be touched with the feeling of our infirmities; but was in all points tempted like as we are, yet without sin. Let us therefore come boldly unto the throne of grace, that we may obtain mercy, and find grace to help in time of need.*

Proverbs 26:27 *Whoso diggeth a pit shall fall therein: and he that rolleth a stone, it will return upon him.*

Proverbs 28:10 *He who leads the upright along the path of evil will fall into his own pit, but the blameless will inherit what is good.*

Ecclesiastes 10:8 *He who digs a pit may fall into it, and he who breaches a wall may be bitten by a snake.*

Please know that when you connect and admonish people who operate in this manner, the blood that is on their hands is now on yours. You are responsible for the bleeding on the altar of God's word that he did not require a sacrifice for, and you are responsible for how you soul tied to someone who was not operating in his fruit, character, motives, or nature. ***Study Ezekiel 3 and Ezekiel 33***.

Isaiah 59:3-8 *For your hands are defiled with blood, and your fingers with iniquity; your lips have spoken lies, your tongue hath muttered perverseness. None calleth for justice, nor any pleadeth for truth: they trust in vanity, and speak lies; they conceive mischief, and bring forth iniquity. They hatch cockatrice' eggs, and weave the spider's web: he that eateth of their eggs dieth, and that which is crushed breaketh out into a viper. Their webs shall not become garments, neither shall they cover themselves with their works: their works are works of iniquity, and the act of violence is in their hands.*

Their feet run to evil, and they make haste to shed innocent blood: their thoughts are thoughts of iniquity; wasting and destruction are in their paths. The way of peace they know not; and there is no judgment in their goings: they have made them crooked paths: whosoever goeth therein shall not know peace.

We only can shed blood that God is requiring and in the way he is requiring. We cannot shed innocent blood, nor can we inflict further harm upon people that God is judging. He is doing the judging, not us. We are just conduits. He sits one down and puts up another, not us. He defends and not really defends but reveals the truth and reality of his word to those he is speaking to and onlookers, not us. Our posture is to stand and see the salvation of the Lord.

Exodus 14:13-14 *And Moses said unto the people, Fear ye not, stand still, and see the salvation of the Lord, which he will shew to you to day: for the Egyptians whom ye have seen to day, ye shall see them again no more for ever.*

Psalm 40:10-11 *Be still, and know that I am God: I will be exalted among the heathen, I will be exalted in the earth. The Lord of hosts is with us; the God of Jacob is our refuge. Selah.*

2Chronicles 20:17 *Ye shall not need to fight in this battle: set yourselves, stand ye still, and see the salvation of the LORD with you, O Judah and Jerusalem: fear not, nor be dismayed; to morrow go out against them: for the LORD will be with you.*

Operating from a godly posture that exalts and edifies him, will allow you to draw and save more souls which is God's ultimate intent and purpose of man – that they might be saved and live in eternal life with him.

John 3:16 *For God so loved the world, that he gave his only Son, that whoever believes in him should not perish but have eternal life.*

As you share your traumas with God, endeavor to exchange them for his truth and healing power.

This is essential so that you will not dread being used of him and so that you can remain grounded in an unwavering stance of righteousness for him. Jeremiah the prophet constantly shared with God how hurt he was by his experiences. Jeremiah was saying things I would not have the guts to say to God. But it was his truth that he was exchanging for God's truth. God had to continuously restore him in God identity, wellness, and truth. Go to God continuously so that you can decrease, and he can increase on the inside of you.

OVERTHROWING ALTARS & DEMONIC KINGDOMS

Some of the revelation in this chapter is from my manual, "*The Great Awakening; Igniting Regional Revival*" and "*Gatekeeping Regions For God's Glory*." In ***Genesis 1:28,*** God gave man dominion over every sphere of influence in the earth. This influence was over animals, the sea and sea creatures, the land, the air, kingdoms, regions, and nations, etc. We were to rule over everything.

And God blessed them, and God said unto them, Be fruitful, and multiply, and replenish the earth, and subdue it: and have dominion over the fish of the sea, and over the fowl of the air, and over every living thing that moveth upon the earth.

Demons are all about housing themselves in realms and spheres and desolate places that we fail to inhabit. In these regions, they establish their kingdoms, establish worship, and sacrifice on demonic altars, gather to discuss their plans, gain and store intel on their prey, and dispatch demons, legalities, curses, witchcraft, and demonic assignments against people, regions, lands, and atmospheres.

Dictionary.com defines *altar* as:

1. an elevated place or structure, as a mound or platform, at which religious rites are performed or on which sacrifices are offered to gods, ancestors, etc."
2. a table or flat-topped block used as the focus for a religious ritual, especially for making sacrifices or offerings to a deity

Wikipedia defines altars (Hebrew: *mizbe'ah*) "*a place of slaughter or sacrifice.*"

Biblestudytools.com states that particularly in the Old Testament*: altars were places where the divine and human worlds interacted. Altars were places of exchange, communication, and influence. God responded actively to altar activity.* Altars were a place of worship, sacrifice, atonement, and redemption. The God of the altar governed your life and offered safety, health, wealth, and happiness in exchange for your worship and sacrifice.

Depending on what is being conducted, altars can be a curse or a blessing ***(Numbers 23:1-30)***.

- ✓ Altars release generational inheritance and even the fate of generations. They can speak and establish the personal and generational fate of destinies and what god controls that destiny. ***(Genesis 28:11-22, Genesis 32)***

- ✓ Altars operate as memorials and sacred dedicated grounds. ***(Genesis 17:15-21, Genesis 22:15-18, 1 Samuel 7:8-12)***

- ✓ Altars can speak on your behalf, either negatively or positively, in your absence or presence. Why? Because there is a deity behind the altar. ***(Revelation 16:7)***

- ✓ What is sacrificed on an altar determines what is produced and released from that altar. Such sacrifices are tied to dedications, vows, and covenants that are made through a spiritual legal agreement. These legal agreements can be for life and require some form of payment to break them. Many demonic altars require blood, murder, or death to break dedications, vows, and covenants. They also retaliate with vengeance, torment, and death attacks when people no longer want to serve at their altars.

- ✓ Altars provide supernatural access that can be used divinely or demonically. They can serve as gateways, portals, and access points that open and connect to ley lines, highways, and entryways in dream realms and spiritual realms. Depending on the altar, demons, angels, Godly people, witches, warlocks, wicked, and ignorant people can use these supernatural realms to access people, places, and things. ***(1Kings 17:1; 18:1-45)***

In the New Testament, Jesus became the ultimate sacrifice, therefore the stationary altar became a moving platform where we can now trade in worship and sacrifice with God through relationship with him.

We, therefore, see that platform is not just a constructed area but is any avenue where a person can voice an agenda, expose an agenda, or pursue an agenda for a particular purpose. When these agendas are released, it serves as a sacrifice being offered unto the altar of that platform. The purpose or origin of that agenda determines what god is being sacrificed upon that altar. A transaction then occurs between the person and that god to which that altar belongs. Thus, a person trades what they are sacrificing for what that deity is releasing in their life through that agenda.

Even if a person says they serve the true and living God, there is no way to agree, sacrifice unto, or sow into an altar that does not serve his kingdom agenda and still contend he or she is not serving an idol god. The person has resorted to strange fire and mixture whether they want to admit it or not. God does not receive strange fire no matter how much we contend our sacrifice is to him.

When we consider altars, especially demonic altars, we tend to think they are built in a specific location, and we must actually go to that location to offer up a sacrifice. However, it is important to realize that altars can be movable trading floors and platforms.

Altars can also be high places within the earth realm, spiritual realms, and demonic kingdom.

Scouts, it is so important to know the intel below as these are the regions, spheres, and atmospheres you need to claim and assert sonship authority in and over. You will need to understand how people, lands, atmospheres, regions, and nations are tied to demonic altars within these terrains.

- ❑ ***Second Heaven*** – Principalities, territorial strongholds, rulers & powers

- ❑ ***Spiritual Wickedness In High Place*s** - Cults, shrines, covens, altars, altars in retail stores and marketplace services, homes, backrooms, psychic shops, yoga spots, exercise agencies that do yoga, martial arts, pilates, etc; witchcraft shops, idolatrous lands, atmospheres, buildings, and organizations, planned parenthood, abortion clinics

- ❑ ***Prince Of The Power Of The Air*** - Allergies, pollens, viruses, bacterial infections, airborne pathogens, pestilences, famines, social media spheres, internet realms and spheres, atmospheric realms

- ***Mountains Spheres Of Influence*** - Education, religion, family, business, politics, government, military, arts/entertainment, media, technology, artificial intelligence

- ***Kingdoms Of This World*** – Carnality, perversion, trafficking, mammon, idolatry, cultural trends, fear mongering; mountains spheres of influence works with and within the kingdoms of this world

- ***Specialize Witchcraft Practitioners & Witchcraft Workings*** – Witchcraft workings being done to the moon, constellations, stars, sun, galaxies, universe, atmospheres, climates, earth elements

- ***Idolatrous Organizations*** – Transactional altar, blood through oaths, blood sacrifices, hazing, ritualistic abuse, Stockholm syndrome, blood rituals

- ***Marine Kingdom*** – Under the waters - major uprising in this kingdom – pedophilia, Mayan voodoo priest rituals, Native American rituals, kingdom financers

  (*Sidebar Revelation:* If you have household wickedness in your bloodline that is tied to waters, or if you live in regions that have bodies of water or lots of rivers lakes, ponds, etc., or if you have lots of night season and dream realm activity regarding the marine kingdom, witchcraft tied to the marine kingdom, etc, you must govern in this area and assert the authority God has given you and your bloodline in this area. Assert your jurisdiction over bodies of water that God reveals to you in these areas and over pipelines).

- ❑ ***Animal Kingdom*** - Sacrifices to animals, tribal spirits, ancestral spirit guides, shapeshifting demons and workings, black magic, Santeria witchcraft workings, dream realm attacks where demonic animals are connected to this kingdom

- ❑ ***Kingdom Of The Forest*** – Demonic fires, shadows and shadowy figures and spirits, demonic and creature sightings, witchcraft connected to trees, flowers, plants, greens; many hidden or side lash attacks can come from the forests

- ❑ ***Dry Places & Desserts*** – Strongman spirits wander to dry places then seek to return to their hosts bringing seven more demons back with them; Native American and African witchcraft are tied to these kingdoms; dinosaurs, scorpions, druids, snake spirits and demonic workings are rooted in these regions

- ❑ ***Sheol & the Grave*** – Graves, coffins, abode of the dead, hades dungeons, lower death regions, suicidal and depressed regions

- ❑ ***Gates Of Hell*** – Hell itself, realms around, or within hell, realms of the dead, realms of eternal judgement and damnation

Ephesians 6:12 *For we wrestle not against flesh and blood, but against principalities, against powers, against the rulers of the darkness of this world, against spiritual wickedness in high places.*

Ephesians 2:24 *Wherein in time past ye walked according to the course of this world, according to the prince of the power of the air, the spirit that now worketh in the children of disobedience:"*

Ezekiel 26:15-21 *Thus saith the Lord GOD to Tyrus; Shall not the isles shake at the sound of thy fall, when the wounded cry, when the slaughter is made in the midst of thee? Then all the princes of the sea shall come down from their thrones, and lay away their robes, and put off their broidered garments: they shall clothe themselves with trembling; they shall sit upon the ground, and shall tremble at every moment, and be astonished at thee. And they shall take up a lamentation for thee, and say to thee, How art thou destroyed, that wast inhabited of seafaring men, the renowned city, which wast strong in the sea, she and her inhabitants, which cause their terror to be on all that haunt it! Now shall the isles tremble in the day of thy fall; yea, the isles that are in the sea shall be troubled at thy departure. For thus saith the Lord GOD; When I shall make thee a desolate city, like the cities that are not inhabited; when I shall bring up the deep upon thee, and great waters shall cover thee; When I shall bring thee down with them that descend into the pit, with the people of old time, and shall set thee in the low parts of the earth, in places desolate of old, with them that go down to the pit, that thou be not* *inhabited; and I shall set glory in the land of the living; I will make thee a terror, and thou shalt be no more: though thou be sought for, yet shalt thou never be found again, saith the Lord GOD.*

Philippians 2:10 *That at the name of Jesus every knee should bow, of those in heaven, and of those on earth, and of those under the earth.*

Luke 11:24-26 *When the unclean spirit is gone out of a man, he walketh through dry places, seeking rest; and finding none, he saith, I will return unto my house whence I came out. And when he cometh, he findeth it swept and garnished. Then goeth he, and taketh to him seven other spirits more wicked than himself; and they enter in, and dwell there: and the last state of that man is worse than the first.*

Revelation 11:15 *Then the seventh angel sounded: And there were loud voices in heaven, saying, "The kingdoms of this world have become the kingdoms of our Lord and of His Christ, and He shall reign forever and ever!"*

Daniel 7:15-28 speaks of the animal kingdom and also the overtaking of the kingdoms of this world by God's kingdom.

Revelation 12:12 *Therefore rejoice, ye heavens, and ye that dwell in them. Woe to the inhabiters of the earth and of the sea! for the devil is come down unto you, having great wrath, because he knoweth that he hath but a short time.*

The soul, lands, atmospheres, and regions can be so sinful or damaged that it can literally feel like the person, place, or thing, are in hell even though it is right here on earth.

Psalm 139:7-14 The Amplified Bible *Where could I go from Your Spirit? Or where could I flee from Your presence? If I ascend up into heaven, You are there; if I make my bed in Sheol (the place of the dead), behold, You are there. If I take the wings of the morning or dwell in the uttermost parts of the sea, Even there shall Your hand lead me, and Your right hand shall hold me.*

If I say, Surely the darkness shall cover me and the night shall be [the only] light about me, Even the darkness hides nothing from You, but the night shines as the day; the darkness and the light are both alike to You. For You did form my inward parts; You did knit me together in my mother's womb. I will confess and praise You for You are fearful and wonderful and for the awful wonder of my birth! Wonderful are Your works, and that my inner self knows right well.

Psalm 86:13 *For great is thy mercy toward me: and thou hast delivered my soul from the lowest hell.*

Psalm 16:10 *For You will not abandon my soul to Sheol; Nor will You allow Your Holy One to undergo decay.*

Psalm 30:3 *O LORD, You have brought up my soul from Sheol; You have kept me alive, that I would not go down to the pit.*

Job 11:7-10 *Can you find out the deep things of God, or can you by searching find out the limits of the Almighty [explore His depths, ascend to His heights, extend to His breadths, and comprehend His infinite perfection]? His wisdom is as high as the heights of heaven! What can you do? It is deeper than Sheol (the place of the dead)! What can you know? Longer in measure [and scope] is it than the earth, and broader than the sea. If [God] sweeps in and arrests and calls into judgment, who can hinder Him? [If He is against a man, who shall call Him to account for it?]*

Hosea 13:14 *Shall I ransom them from the power of Sheol? Shall I redeem them from death? O Death, where are your thorns? O Sheol, where is your sting? Compassion will be hidden from My sight.*

Psalm 56:13 *For You have delivered my soul from death, Indeed my feet from stumbling, So that I may walk before God In the light of the living.*

Job 38:17 *Have the gates of death been opened unto thee? or hast thou seen the doors of the shadow of death? Hast thou perceived the breadth of the earth? declare if thou knowest it all.*

Isaiah 38:10 *I said in the cutting off of my days, I shall go to the gates of the grave: I am deprived of the residue of my years.*

Matthew 16:17 *And I say also unto thee, That thou art Peter, and upon this rock I will build my church; and the gates of hell shall not prevail against it.*

Romans 8:37-39 *No, in all these things we are more than conquerors through him who loved us. For I am convinced that neither death nor life, neither angels nor demons, neither the present nor the future, nor any powers, neither height nor depth, nor anything else in all creation, will be able to separate us from the love of God that is in Christ Jesus our Lord.*

<u>Indicators that a person, place, or thing maybe in hell:</u>

- It feels like you are experiencing or living in hell on earth.
- It feels like death or someone or something is dying.
- When there is a desire to die but no reason to die.
- When there is the presence of sabotage, premature death, or suicide.
- When there is an aura of extreme hopelessness, helplessness, loneliness, dejection, rejection, and depression.
- When there is a dullness that hinders praise, worship, exaltation, or serving of God.
- When there is an aura of darkness and oppression.

- When there is affliction due to the oppression that is manifesting.
- When a feeling of seizing into doom and depression is in operation.
- When everything looks dark and gloomy, or it is as if everything is dying or not working.
- When there is a sensation or impression of being exiled.
- When there is an impression of extreme judgment and condemnation that feels like torture or torment. This can be in general or due to unrepented sin.
- When there is the operation of extreme sin and a lack of conviction for unholiness.

1Corinthians 15:55 *O death, where is thy sting? O grave, where is thy victory?*

Hosea 13:14 *Shall I ransom them from the power of Sheol? Shall I redeem them from death? O Death, where are your thorns? O Sheol, where is your sting? Compassion will be hidden from My sight.*

There are trading floors in the natural realm right among us that we must open our eyes to. Some of the little unassuming shops and restaurants are some of the biggest trading floors for witchcraft and idolatry. Especially psychic readings businesses, yoga studios, tattoo parlors, night clubs, sex shops, culture and ethnic focused herbal shops, restaurants with Buddhist and other idolatrous themes. Major witchcraft is being released into the region, as sacrifices and trading services are occurring by people unto idol gods.

TV, commercials, social media, the internet, ad displays at stores, clothing, your job, etc., are all trading floor platforms. They are all altars designed to get our attention and get us to buy into and trade our time, money, morals, beliefs, destiny, life, heritage, etc. for their product. Sadly, because these platforms are self-serving altars or demonic altars, if we are not careful, we can open gateways for idolatry, pornography, perversion, and the Anti-Christ agenda to constantly seep into our lives. Depending on what we take in and give ourselves to, we resort to sacrificing unto idol gods and trading the hedge of God for demonic attacks and influences of the enemy.

Moreover, if we have platforms in these arenas, we must make sure our platform is rooted in God, such that what we promote and release, glorifies and offers up sacrifices unto him. For example, your Facebook page is a platform. What you like, comment on, share, write, and allow on your page, determines what God you are sacrificing unto at the time. Because there is so much being released on Facebook, many tend to have a lot of mixture and be desensitized to many videos, statuses, pictures, etc. that do not glorify God. We must be careful that our likes, shares, and comments have not given way to trading on altars that are not of God. It is also important to be careful that we do not yield our page to idolatry, pornography, and perversion.

We do not realize it, but when we are watching things on TV or listening to vile music that is rooted in perversion and idolatry, we are sacrificing our purity, dream and sleep realm unto idolatry. Such platforms are designed to confuse and desensitize us to sin and wickedness. This gives demons the avenue to fill us with lustful thoughts and desires, sexually molest and rape us as we sleep and dream, elude us to compromising the word of God and make light of issues that hold us in bondage. A trade occurs on the altar whether we like it or not, whether we acknowledge it or not, whether we agree to it or not. It is a platform; therefore, it is an altar where transactions are being made between you and that agenda.

Examples of trading in the bible:

- Adam and Eve traded eternal life for the knowledge of good and evil (***Genesis 3:6).***
- Esau traded his birthright, inheritance, and destiny, for food (***Genesis 25:29-34).***
- Jezebel, an idolatrous descendent, usurped the authority of her husband and God to gain control over her region and the people (***1Kings, 2Kings, Revelations 20:20***).
- Athaliah traded the life and lineage of her grandkids by killing them so she could be heir to the throne (***2Kings 11).***
- Samson traded his purity and the secret of his strength for sex and the heart of a woman (***Judges 16:6***).
- Judas traded his apostolic calling and relationship with Jesus for money (***Matthew 26:27***).

- Leviathan, the king of pride, is a trading floor that operates under the waters. He also operates in the airway through communication and self-exaltation. People willingly and ignorantly trade on these floors for self-glory, to control the airway, communication systems, and patterns. Leviathan is a huge trading floor among social media sites and the World Wide Web. It is also huge among people who want to be ruling leaders in their spheres of influence. (***Psalms 74:14, Psalms 104:26, Job 3:8, Job 41, Isaiah 27:10***).

- A Lukewarm gospel is a trading floor. We are trading at idolatrous altars when we preach the word in error or make light of sin and iniquity (***Ezekiel 3:18-20, Ezekiel 33:6-9, 2Timothy 2:3-5, James 1:22, Revelations 3:15-17***).

- When we trade God's will, standards, and laws, for the world's ways or for our own knowledge, we are trading on demonic floors (***Proverbs 3:7, Proverbs 4:19-21, Romans 12:2, James 3:15-17***).

- Murder is a trading floor in and of itself. We see this with stories of Cain and Abel, John the Baptist, Jesus, Stephen, and other apostles killed for the gospel (***Genesis 4, Deuteronomy 23:43, Psalms 79:10, Luke 23:26-42, Mark 6:14-29, Acts 7:54-60, Revelations 6:9-11***) These deaths are of people with great calls on their lives. These murders can be senseless as witches and warlocks will release prayers for senseless murders as a way of offering up sacrifices to idols. We are experiencing this in a lot of regions with high crime rates. The blood of the innocent crying from the land as they are sacrifices to idols for whatever reason. A lot of ancient spirits from tribal times are resurfacing in regions and are the root of gang culture, and turf wars. Such crimes are senseless murders being used as sacrifices offered to idols.

- Abortion is a murderous trading floor. The bible speaks about not allowing children to pass through the fire. We think that it's ok because it is a law-abiding clinic. But that clinic is a demonic altar where kids are traded and sacrificed to idols of Molech, Ammon, etc. (***Leviticus 18:21, Deuteronomy 18:10, Deuteronomy 12:31, 2Kings 6:2-3, 2Kings 17:16-17, 2Kings 23:10, 2Chronicles 33:6, Psalms 106, 37-38, Jeremiah 7:30-31, Ezekiel 23:27-29***).

- Israel traded and worshipped Sidon gods – Baal, Ashtaroth, Moab, gods of Syria, gods of the Ammonites, and the gods of the Philistines on the trading floor seaports of Tyre and Sidon (***Judges 1:31, Judges 10:6-10, 1Kings 16:31, Isaiah 23, Jeremiah 25, Ezekiel 26-28, Amos 1:9-10, Zechariah 9:1-4).***

  Jesus teaches about how Tyre and Sidon would have been saved long ago, had the saints dealt with the high places and trading floors (***Matthew 15-21-28, Luke 10:13-14, Mark3:7-8***).

Many regions with large bodies of water have underground trading floors in their waters. People who desire high level platforms within government, entertainment, notorious drug lords, gang members, mafia members, etc., willingly seek mediums and offer sacrifices to these trading floors, in exchange for power, finances, prestige, and success. People within the region who are under the bondages of principalities and territorial spirits in the underworld, willingly and ignorantly offer up sacrifices to these demonic trading floors.

We must be careful with where we personally trade, the ministry trades, the saints trade, and where those within the region are trading as it relates to altars. We must watch where we are trading because we are buying more than just entertainment or a nice product. We could be trading with an idol god who eventually is going to want more than what the trade was worth. We could be trading to an idolatrous trading floor and further strengthening the powers of darkness against our lives, destinies, generational line, and the body of Christ. It is important to seek God in discerning trading floors in the spiritual realms in and around our region and to ask for revelation regarding the major principalities that rule them. Through warfare, intercession, a drawing the people into repentance, cleansing of the land and atmosphere, planting godly businesses, services, etc., within the region, these principalities and powers can be displaced, and their trading floors shut down while establishing the kingdom of God in the earth.

Sometimes demonic altars and trading floors have to be dealt with in the court of heaven, especially if they have a generational bondage connected to them. Many of us are not made aware of the generational demonic altars we are tied to until we come under extreme spiritual warfare and pursue reasons the enemy has legal rights over our lives. Holy Spirit or tracing generational patterns of iniquity lead us to realizing we are dealing with a legal binding to a demonic altar. Many dedications and covenants are made to demonic altars through witchcraft practices or idolatrous organizations. People are seeking protection, success, love, money, fame, belonging, and advancement. They sale themselves and their generational line to the devil for a potion, power, or divine assistance.

I cannot tell you how many dedications and covenants I have had to break off people because family members sold their future generations to idols. Evil altars track, harass, and torment these people in an effort to get them to pay and succumb to debts their ancestors made. I have aided in bringing deliverance where people's identities, gifts, destiny, callings, virtue, womb, reproductive and sexual organs, offspring, finances, ability to be married, and success was sold to the devil. People were dedicated and married to demons and did not know it. Or they were dedicated and sold to the devil such that they were expected to live for him – be a queen or king in his kingdom and use their gifts and callings for him. These people live hard lives of spiritual harassment as demons track them throughout life and in their dream realm in effort to create scenarios where they live for the devil. When they desire to be saved, the wrath of hell comes against them. They are raped, molested, abused, targeted, and tormented, all because they want to live for God rather than the devil. They are made to pay with their lives for decisions that were made for them by their ancestors. Until they assert their right to verbally renounce and break the dedications and covenants, and war for freedom through the blood of Jesus Christ and his finished works on the cross, they are bound by these attacks in their sleep and dream realm and throughout their life.

Many people do not even know they are to break these dedications and covenants. Imagine how many people have died from the wrath of demonic systems because they resisted or rejected a generational dedication and covenant that was made to a demonic altar on their behalf. Many within the body of Christ do not believe in or consistently practice the deliverance ministry of casting out devils, so they know nothing about needing to break people free from demonic altars. I would not know about it had the Holy Spirit not revealed it to me as I went through a season of deliverance and as I had aided others in being delivered. And even then, I have only heard of minimal revelation on the matter. I have had to rely on the Holy Spirit to assist people with how to shut down these heartless, relentless, vengeful attacks and predatory assignments. The bible clearly reveals to us the truth about our sins, iniquities, and transgressions. Especially those related to idolatry.

Exodus 34:7 *Keeping mercy for thousands, forgiving iniquity and transgression and sin, and that will by no* *means clear the guilty; visiting (punishing) the iniquity of the fathers upon the children, and upon the children's children, unto the third and to the fourth generation.*

Dictionary.com defines *iniquity* as, *"gross injustice, wickedness, wicked act, a violation of right or duty."*

Depending on where we fall in the bloodline and whether previous generations served Jesus Christ, we can either inherit great blessings, or great pain. The cross provides an avenue for these iniquities to be nullified from one generation to the next. However, somebody has to rise up in the family line as a curse breaker and make sure the guilty iniquities are cleared. When there is no righteous seed contending for the bloodline, generational iniquity reigns and lands on innocent generations. They are paying for the sins of their mothers, fathers, and previous generations.

Psalm 11 *In the Lord put I my trust: how say ye to my soul, Flee as a bird to your mountain? For, lo, the wicked bend their bow, they make ready their arrow upon the string, that they may privily shoot at the upright in heart. If the foundations be destroyed, what can the righteous do? The Lord is in his holy temple, the Lord's throne is in heaven: his eyes behold, his eyelids try, the children of men. The Lord trieth the righteous: but the wicked and him that loveth violence his soul hateth. Upon the wicked he shall rain snares, fire and brimstone, and a horrible tempest: this shall be the portion of their cup. For the* *righteous Lord loveth righteousness; his countenance doth behold the upright.*

What a gross injustice to pay for a sin you did not even commit. **The generational foundation is faulty so the innocent and even the righteous reap the demise of their ancestors.** This is how much God hates sin. He established a biblical law through ***Exodus*** 34:7, where the consequences of sin can last for generations and fall upon innocent generations. God will not violate this law even though he sent Jesus to give us victory over the judgment of the law. But we have to receive Jesus Christ as our personal savior, serve and live for him, and assert our right to be free from personal and generational iniquity. We correct our iniquities through repentance and our right to be delivered through the blood of Jesus Christ and his finished works of the cross.
Lamentations 5:7 Our fathers sinned, and are no more; it is we who have borne their iniquities.

Sometimes demons will not adhere to us verbally breaking the curse, renouncing idols, nullifying dedications, and covenants that are tied to demonic altars. They will continue to harass us until a legal judgment is released to restrain them from making us pay a debt that came through a sacrifice to a demonic altar. They will send constant fiery darts that are designed to destroy us. It will be a sieging experience as we are flamed on every side and feel trapped inside the terror of this demonic confederacy.

LET'S PAUSE – SELAH – ON THIS REVELATION FOR A MOMENT!

Shift Right Now!

<u>Judging Demonic Altars In The Courts Of Heaven:</u>

- ❑ Call courts and summon the demons tied to the altar that are tracking and attacking you.
- ❑ Repent for sin done on the altar personally and generationally.
- ❑ Renounce the personal and generational idol gods, dedications, vows, and covenants as it relates to the altar.
- ❑ Ask Jesus Christ to break the legal covenants, nullify the legal charges as it relates to sacrifices made to that altar, and to judge the systems and demonic spirits tied to these altars.
- ❑ Ask Jesus Christ to release a divine restraining order.
- ❑ Identify, shut down, cast out, and break the powers tied to trading floors, demonic kingdoms, and altars.
- ❑ Destroy anything connected to this altar.
- ❑ If you are tied to this altar through an organization, submit a written notice dissolving your association and membership with that organization.
- ❑ Ask Jesus Christ to reestablish you and your generational line back in right standing with the covenant of God and his altar.

GOVERNING LANDS, SPHERES, REGIONS, NATIONS

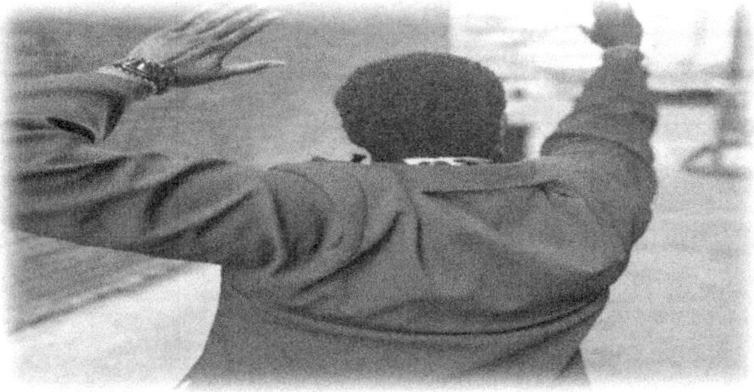

This revelation includes keys for properly **GOVERNING & CLAIMING** lands, seas, spheres, regions, and nations. These keys will mostly entail scriptural passages to help you discern the biblical principles of governing and claiming territories. Embodying the scriptures are vital to you recognizing that this is your sonship right and inheritance as a child of God.

Govern from Dictionary.com means:

1. to rule over by right of authority
2. to exercise a directing or restraining influence over; guide
3. to hold in check; control
4. to serve as or constitute a law for
5. to be regularly accompanied by or require the use of
6. to regulate the speed
7. to exercise the function of government
8. to have predominating influence

Governing is about operating and CLAIMING the dominion of sonship as kingdom heirs of the throne and inheritance of God.

Genesis 1:28 *And God blessed them, and God said unto them, Be fruitful, and multiply, and replenish the earth, and subdue it: and have dominion over the fish of the sea, and over the fowl of the air, and over every living thing that moveth upon the earth.*

Son of God, be:

- ✓ **Fruitful (para)** – Bear fruit literally or figuratively, bear, bring forth, cause to be, grow, increase, to show fruitfulness.

- ✓ **Multiply (raba)** – Increase in abundance, bring up, enlarge, excel, exceed, grow up, heap, nourish, multiply with plenty, store, thoroughly increase, shoot up.

- ✓ **Replenish** (malae)– To fill, be full of, fulfill, fill the hand, be ended, accomplish, confirm, consecrate, satisfy, have wholly.

- ✓ **Subdue (kanas)** – To negatively disregard, tread down, to conquer, subjugate, violate, bring to bondage, force, keep under, bring into subjection, make subservient, dominate.

Dominion Over:

- The fish of the sea – All bodies of water; rivers, lakes, oceans, seas, animals in the sea; demons, entities, activities, kingdoms, and trading floors under the waters.

  (*Sidebar Revelation:* If you have household wickedness in your bloodline that is tied to waters, or if you live in regions that have bodies of water or lots of rivers lakes, ponds, etc., or if you have lots of night season and dream realm activity regarding the marine kingdom, witchcraft tied to the marine kingdom, etc, you must govern in this area and assert the authority God has given you and your bloodline in this area. Assert your jurisdiction over bodies of water that God reveals to you in these areas and over pipelines).

- The fowl of the air – Air, wind, atmospheres, environments, frequencies, airways, dream realms, spiritual realms and spheres, regions, flying animals, flying entities, astral projectors, translators, demons, angels, heaven.

- Every living thing that moveth upon the earth – **ANYTHING THAT MOVES! CATCH THAT IN THE SPIRIT!** Lands, mountains, terrains, forests, desserts, communities, regions, nations, mankind, demons, systems, worldly and demonic kingdoms and regions.

Dominion in Hebrew *râdâ* and means:

1. to tread down, i.e. subjugate (to bring under complete control or subjection; conquer; master, submissive, enslave); specifically, to crumble off
2. (come to, make to) have dominion, prevail against, reign, (bear, make to) rule, (over), take
3. to rule, have dominion, dominate, tread down
    a) (Qal) to have dominion, rule, subjugate
    b) (Hiphil) to cause to dominate
    c) to scrape out
    d) (Qal) to scrape, scrape out

Deuteronomy 11:24 *Every place where the sole of your foot treads will be yours. Your territory will extend from the wilderness to Lebanon, and from the Euphrates River to the Western Sea.*

Joshua 1:3-6 *Every place that the sole of your foot shall tread upon, that have I given unto you, as I said unto Moses. From the wilderness and this Lebanon even unto the great river, the river Euphrates, all the land of the Hittites, and unto the great sea toward the going down of the sun, shall be your coast. There shall not any man be able to stand before thee all the days of thy life: as I was with Moses, so I will be with thee: I will not fail thee, nor forsake thee. Be strong and of a good courage: for unto this people shalt thou divide for an inheritance the land, which I sware unto their fathers to give them.*

It is important to tread spiritually and naturally in the territories God has granted to your hands.

Tread in the Hebrew is *dârak* and means:

1. to tread; by implication, to walk
2. also to string a bow (by treading on it in bending)
3. archer (a person who shoots with a bow and arrow; bowman)
4. bend, come, draw, go (over), guide, lead (forth), thresh, tread (down),
5. treader, tread upon, lead, march, march, forth

Luke 10:19 *Behold, I give unto you power to tread on serpents and scorpions, and over all the power of the enemy: and nothing shall by any means hurt you.*

Tread is *pateo* in the Greek and means:

1. to trample, crush with the feet, to advance by setting foot upon, tread upon
2. to encounter successfully the greatest perils from the machinations and persecutions with which Satan would fain thwart the preaching of the gospel
3. to tread under foot, trample on
4. to treat with insult and contempt
5. to desecrate the holy city by devastation and outrage

The lands, seas, spheres, regions, and nations must know and experience the treading of your governance. As you tread, they respond to who God has made you to be in their midst.

Isaiah 49:1-4 *Listen, O isles, unto me; and hearken, ye people, from afar; The Lord hath called me from the womb; from the bowels of my mother hath he made mention of my* *name. And he hath made my mouth like a sharp sword; in the shadow of his hand hath he hid me, and made me a polished shaft; in his quiver hath he hid me; And said unto me, Thou art my servant, O Israel, in whom I will be glorified. Then I said, I have laboured in vain, I have spent my strength for nought, and in vain: yet surely my judgment is with the Lord, and my work with my God.*

New Living Bible *Listen to me, all you in distant lands! Pay attention, you who are far away! The Lord called me before my birth; from within the womb he called me by name. He made my words of judgment as sharp as a sword. He has hidden me in the shadow of his hand. I am like a sharp arrow in his quiver. He said to me, "You are my servant, Israel, and you will bring me glory." I replied, "But my work seems so useless! I have spent my strength for nothing and to no purpose. Yet I leave it all in the Lord's hand; I will trust God for my reward."*

We tend to think that being called means a plan has been set in our lives for the future, but the ***Message Bible*** of this scripture reads:

The Message Bible *Listen, far-flung islands, pay attention, faraway people: God put me to work from the day I was born. The moment I entered the world he named me.*

God put you and me to work from birth! We think destiny started when we became saved or when we begin doing something successful. It has been God's intention that the call on our lives launch us into working for him from the day we left the womb. Sin in the garden altered this plan but Jesus Christ restored it through the redemption of his shed blood and works on the cross.

The scripture says "***Listen, O isles, unto me; and hearken, ye people, from afar.***" That word *isles* in the Hebrew means *region. Listen, O region!* That is a command or mandate proclamation. *Listen, O isles, O region!*

Region is îy in Hebrew and means:

1. properly, a habitable spot (as desirable)
2. dry land, coast, a coast, an island
3. country, isle, island/s, shore, region

Dictionary.com defines *region* as:

1. firmanant, space, area, range, district without boundaries
2. an area of interest, activity, pursuit, etc.; field
3. regions of the mind and body
4. divisions of cities, territories, universe, heavenlies

Listen is *šâma* in Hebrew and means:

1. to hear intelligently and to be obedient
2. listen attentively, carefully, certainly
3. to consent, declare, discern, or give ear
4. to perceive, proclaim, publish, regard, report, to bear witness

The region has ears, and you can command it to listen intelligently. You can command it to be diligently obedient to what you are saying and to respond to what you are decreeing by mandating that it publishes your words while bearing witness by producing the fruit of your words in the region. As you decree, establish, and complete God's work into these regions, the regions declare back to you what you said by producing your words in the land, sea, people, businesses, ministries, organizations, atmosphere, climate, and heavenlies. Or in your specific case, by producing your words concerning your destiny and vision into the earth. These are words that God has already published in the region as the word call is *qârâ'* in the Hebrew and means, "*the idea of accosting a person.*" Accosting means, "*to confront boldly, to approach especially with a greeting.*" *Qara* also means, "*to call out to (i.e. properly, address by name, to call forth, cry (unto), (be) famous, guest, invite, mention, (give) name, preach, (make) proclamation, pronounce, publish.*"

The region knows we are called from birth because God released our destiny into the ears of the region when we were in the womb. He did not just speak it; he cried it out with proclamation such that once we are born, the region can respond to our destiny as we begin to journey in life with God. As God gives you goals, plans, visions, strategies, and decrees to speak and complete in the region, you are awakening his will and purpose that was placed in the region at your birth. How awesome is that?

Hearken is *qâšab* in the Hebrew and means:

1. to prick up the ears, to incline, attend (of ears)
2. to give heed, regard, pay attention, listen, give attention

After you command the region to listen, you can prick the ears of (hearken) the people or your remnant, or those who will gleam from your destiny within the region and command them to listen, regard, attend, pay attention, give attention to you and to what the region is producing through you. As you exalt God through decrees, intercession, and warfare regarding what you speak in the region, God being exalted causes those who need who you are and what you are producing to be drawn to you. It is very important to cleanse out atmospheres about you and just in general because whatever is spoken in that region the region can hear it, and publishes that into its ground and sphere.

Romans 8:19 declares *"for the earnest expectation of the creature waiteth for the manifestation of the sons of God.*

The region is anxiously waiting on us – YOU - so it can manifest the depth of what God has put in it.

English Standard Bible *For we know that the whole creation has been groaning together in the pains of childbirth until now.*

We discern from this scripture that our regions possess heavenly portals that constantly groan - constantly giving birth to our words, prayers, and declarations. These regions are always in a birthing position. ***Genesis 1:28*** declares "*be fruitful and multiply.*" This scripture is not just talking about birthing natural children, but about what can be birthed into the areas to which we have dominion. These regions are always positioned to give birth and to multiply.

They are ready for you to legislate heaven to earth for God's glory.

Joshua 14:12-14 The Amplified Bible *So now, give me this hill country about which the LORD spoke that day, for you heard on that day that the [giant-like] Anakim were there, with great fortified cities; perhaps the LORD will be with me, and I shall drive them out just as the LORD said."*

So Joshua blessed him and gave Hebron to Caleb the son of Jephunneh as an inheritance. Therefore, Hebron became the inheritance of Caleb the son of Jephunneh the Kenizzite to this day, because he followed the LORD, the God of Israel, completely. The name of Hebron was formerly Kiriath-arba [city of Arba]; for Arba was the greatest man among the [giant-like] Anakim. Then the land had rest from war.

CLAIM YOUR MOUNTAINS

As you tread, legislate through the following keys:

Sonship – Kingdom prayers and divine workings must be conducted from a position of your sonship right as a believer who has been delivered, healed, saved, reconciled, restored, and adopted unto salvation.

Ephesians 2:6 *And hath raised us up together, and made us sit together in heavenly places in Christ Jesus.*

Matthew 28:18-19 *Then Jesus came to them and said, 'All authority in heaven and on earth has been given to me. Therefore go and make disciples of all nations, baptizing them in the name of the Father and of the Son and of the Holy Spirit.*

Matthew 10:8 *Heal the sick, cleanse the lepers, raise the dead, cast out devils: freely ye have received, freely give.*

Matthew 18:18-20 *Verily I say unto you, Whatsoever ye shall bind on earth shall be bound in heaven: and whatsoever ye shall loose on earth shall be loosed in heaven. Again I say unto you, That if two of you shall agree on earth as touching any thing that they shall ask, it shall be done for them of my Father which is in heaven. For where two or three are gathered together in my name, there am I in the midst of them.*

John 3:27 *John answered and said, "A man can receive nothing unless it has been given to him from heaven.*

Colossians 3:2 *Set your affection on things above, not on things on the earth.*

Affection in the Greek is *phroneō* and means:

1. to exercise the mind, i.e. entertain or have a sentiment or opinion

2. by implication, to be (mentally) disposed (more or less earnestly in a certain direction)
3. intensively, to interest oneself in (with concern or obedience)
4. set the affection on, (be) care(-ful), (be like, be of one, be of the same, let this) mind(-ed), regard, savour, think

Set is a finite focus and position where you are seeking to be, think, do and speak like Jesus. Every time life, circumstances, people, or demons try to get you to focus on earthly things, you are actively posturing your thoughts, feelings, perceptions, and considerations on things which are godly, and kingdom minded. The criteria for what is godly and heavenly minded can be found through an established heavenly perspective – God realities concerning your life and sonship with him. The more you entertain heaven, the more you will be able to live from this place as a lifestyle.

Philippians 4:8 *Fix your thoughts on what is true, honorable, right, pure, lovely, admirable. Think about things that are excellent and worthy of praise.*

Ephesians 1:3 *Blessed be the God and Father of our Lord Jesus Christ, who has blessed us in Christ with every spiritual blessing in the heavenly realms.*

Matthew 6:33 *But seek ye first the kingdom of God, and his righteousness; and all these things shall be added unto you.*

Pray from a heavenly posture and with a focus on heavenly mandates, revelations, understanding, knowledge, counsel, guidance, goals, strategies, prophecies, provisions, affections, and manifestations.

God's Sovereignty - All prayers no matter what type (i.e. Thanksgiving, praise and worship, spiritual warfare, intercession, repentance, decrees, battering ram prayers, etc.) must be authoritative and prayed from a position of knowing who you are and who God is in his sovereignty. **All kingdom mandates and workings that God calls and destines you to do must be done through his sovereignty.** They must be prayed, established, and released through who God is and not what he does; through whom you are spiritually and supernaturally in God identity and not through your natural limitations and perceptions. This is not about loudness, competing, or comparing yourself to others, but sonship position as one who has dominion and knows they govern in the earth and over their spheres of influence. **(*Genesis 1:28, Job 22:28*)**

Galatians 3:26-29 *For ye are all the children of God by faith in Christ Jesus. For as many of you as have been baptized into Christ have put on Christ. There is neither Jew nor Greek, there is neither bond nor free, there is neither male nor female: for ye are all one in Christ Jesus. And if ye be Christ's, then are ye Abraham's seed, and heirs according to the promise.* *

Romans 8:14-17 *For as many as are led by the Spirit of God, these are sons of God. For you did not receive the* *spirit of bondage again to fear, but you received the Spirit of adoption by whom we cry out, "Abba, Father." The Spirit Himself bears witness with our spirit that we are children of God, and if children, then heirs—heirs of God and joint heirs with Christ, if indeed we suffer with Him, that we may also be glorified together.* *

Romans 8:18-25 *For I reckon that the sufferings of this present time are not worthy to be compared with the glory which shall be revealed in us. For the earnest expectation of the creature waiteth for the manifestation of the sons of God. For the creature was made subject to vanity, not willingly, but by reason of him who hath subjected the same in hope, Because the creature itself also shall be delivered from the bondage of corruption into the glorious liberty of the children of God. For we know that the whole creation groaneth and travaileth in pain together until now. And not only they, but ourselves also, which have the firstfruits of the Spirit, even we ourselves groan within ourselves, waiting for the adoption, to wit, the redemption of our body. For we are saved by hope: but hope that is seen is not hope: for what a man seeth, why doth he yet hope for? But if we hope for that we see not, then do we with patience wait for it.*

1John 3:1-2 *Behold what manner of love the Father has bestowed on us, that we should be called children of God! Therefore the world does not know us, because it did not know Him. Beloved, now we are children of God; and it has not yet been revealed what we shall be, but we know* *that when He is revealed, we shall be like Him, for we shall see Him as He is.*

Psalm 82:6 I *said, "You are gods, And all of you are children of the Most High.*

John 10:34 *Jesus replied, "Is it not written in your Law: 'I have said you are gods?'*
Psalm 8:5 *You made him a little lower than the angels; You crowned him with glory and honor.*

Psalm 82:1 *God presides in the divine assembly; He renders judgment among the gods:*

2Corinthians 6:18 *I will be a Father to you, And you shall be My sons and daughters, says the LORD Almighty.*

Galatians 3:13-14 *Christ redeemed us from the curse of the law by becoming a curse for us, for it is written: "Cursed is everyone who is hung on a pole." He redeemed us in order that the blessing given to Abraham might come to the Gentiles through Christ Jesus, so that by faith we might receive the promise of the Spirit.*

Ephesians 1:3-6 *Blessed be the God and Father of our Lord Jesus Christ, who hath blessed us with all spiritual blessings in heavenly places in Christ: According as he hath chosen us in him before the foundation of the world, that we should be holy and without blame before him in love: Having predestinated us unto the adoption of children* *by Jesus Christ to himself, according to the good pleasure of his will, To the praise of the glory of his grace, wherein he hath made us accepted in the beloved. **

Hebrews 2:10-11 *For it was fitting for Him, for whom are all things and by whom are all things, in bringing many sons to glory, to make the captain of their salvation perfect through sufferings. For both He who sanctifies and those who are being sanctified are all of one, for which reason He is not ashamed to call them brethren.*

Isaiah 45:11 *Thus says the LORD, The Holy One of Israel, and his Maker: Ask Me of things to come concerning My sons; And concerning the work of My hands, you command Me.*

Hosea 1:10 *Yet the number of the children of Israel shall be as the sand of the sea, Which cannot be measured or numbered. And it shall come to pass In the place where it was said to them, ' You are not My people, there it shall be said to them, You are sons of the living God.'*

Hosea 11:10 *They shall walk after the LORD. He will roar like a lion. When He roars, then His sons shall come trembling from the west.*

Romans 9:26 *And it shall come to pass in the place where it was said to them,' You are not My people,' There they shall be called sons of the living God.'*

Hebrews 12:5-8 *And you have forgotten the exhortation which speaks to you as to sons: "My son, do not despise the chastening of the LORD, nor be discouraged when you are rebuked by Him; For whom the LORD loves He chastens, and scourges every son whom He receives.' If you endure chastening, God deals with you as with sons; for what son is there whom a father does not chasten? But if you are without chastening, of which all have become partakers, then you are illegitimate and not sons.*

Exalt Jesus Christ & His Works On The Cross – Jesus Christ and his works on the cross has paid every sin and debt for us, such that we are restored unto salvation as if there was never a fall of mankind. Jesus restored us as joint heirs with him. We legislate sonship through his redemptive blood, works on the cross, and the resurrection power of the Holy Spirit.

- ✓ ***Declare the authority and name of Jesus Christ*** – Jesus is the name that gives us the authority to govern over EVERYTHING!

  Matthew 28:18-19 *Then Jesus came to them and said, 'All authority in heaven and on earth has been given to me. Therefore go and make disciples of all nations, baptizing them in the name of the Father and of the Son and of the Holy Spirit.* *

  John 14:13-14 *And whatsoever ye shall ask in my name, that will I do, that the Father may be* *glorified in the Son. If ye shall ask any thing in my name, I will do it. **

Philippians 2:11 *Let this mind be in you, which was also in Christ Jesus: Who, being in the form of God, thought it not robbery to be equal with God: But made himself of no reputation, and took upon him the form of a servant, and was made in the likeness of men: And being found in fashion as a man, he humbled himself, and became obedient unto death, even the death of the cross. Wherefore God also hath highly exalted him, and given him a name which is above every name: That at the name of Jesus every knee should bow, of things in heaven, and things in earth, and things under the earth; And that every tongue should confess that Jesus Christ is Lord, to the glory of God the Father. **

Philippians 2:9-11 *Wherefore God also hath highly exalted him, and given him a name which is above every name: That at the name of Jesus every knee should bow, of things in heaven, and things in earth, and things under the earth; And that every tongue should confess that Jesus Christ is Lord, to the glory of God the Father. **

John 6:36 *He that believeth on the Son hath everlasting life: and he that believeth not the Son shall not see life; but the wrath of God abideth on him.*

Ephesians 1:17-23 *That the God of our Lord Jesus Christ, the Father of glory, may give unto you the spirit of wisdom and revelation in the knowledge of him: The eyes of your understanding being enlightened; that ye may know what is the hope of his calling, and what the riches of the glory of his inheritance in the saints, And what is the exceeding greatness of his power to us-ward who believe, according to the working of his mighty power, Which he wrought in Christ, when he raised him from the dead, and set him at his own right hand in the heavenly places, Far above all principality, and power, and might, and dominion, and every name that is named, not only in this world, but also in that which is to come: And hath put all things under his feet, and gave him to be the head over all things to the church, Which is his body, the fulness of him that filleth all in all.*

Ephesians 2:4-10 *But God, who is rich in mercy, for his great love wherewith he loved us, Even when we were dead in sins, hath quickened us together with Christ, (by grace ye are saved;) And hath raised us up together, and made us sit together in heavenly places in Christ Jesus: That in the ages to come he might shew the exceeding riches of his grace in his kindness toward us through Christ Jesus. For by grace are ye saved through faith; and that not of yourselves: it is the gift of God: Not of works, lest any man should boast. For we are his workmanship, created in Christ Jesus unto good* *works, which God hath before ordained that we should walk in them.*

Titus 2:11-15 *For the grace of God that bringeth salvation hath appeared to all men, Teaching us that, denying ungodliness and worldly lusts, we should live soberly, righteously, and godly, in this present world; Looking for that blessed hope, and the glorious appearing of the great God and our Saviour Jesus Christ; Who gave himself for us, that he might redeem us from all iniquity, and purify unto himself a peculiar people, zealous of good works. These things speak, and exhort, and rebuke with all authority. Let no man despise thee.*

- ✓ ***Apply The Blood of Jesus Christ*** – The Blood of Jesus Christ purges, purifies, redeems, reconciles, sanctifies, sanitizes, forgives, heals, and frees you from death. We hear a lot about pleading the blood, but the blood is an application. You can apply and soak in the blood of Jesus Christ and command purity, cleansing, perfecting, redemption, life, and wholeness to come.

  Ephesians 1:7 *In Him we have redemption through His blood, the forgiveness of sins, according to the riches of His grace. Passover story in* ***Exodus 12***. *

- ✓ ***Works On The Cross*** - Assert your right to be delivered, healed, set free, and towering in victorious dominion through the crucifixion and God's resurrection power.

Romans 10:9 *If you declare with your mouth, 'Jesus is Lord,' and believe in your heart that God raised him from the dead, you will be saved.* *

Colossians 2:12-15 *Buried with him in baptism, wherein also ye are risen with him through the faith of the operation of God, who hath raised him from the dead. And you, being dead in your sins and the uncircumcision of your flesh, hath he quickened together with him, having forgiven you all trespasses; Blotting out the handwriting of ordinances that was against us, which was contrary to us, and took it out of the way, nailing it to his cross; And having spoiled principalities and powers, he made a shew of them openly, triumphing over them in it.*

The Amplified Bible *[Thus you were circumcised when] you were buried with Him in [your] baptism, in which you were also raised with Him [to a new life] through [your] faith in the working of God [as displayed] when He raised Him up from the dead. And you who were dead in trespasses and in the uncircumcision of your flesh (your sensuality, your sinful carnal nature), [God] brought to life together with [Christ], having [freely] forgiven us all our transgressions, Having cancelled and blotted out and wiped away the handwriting of the note (bond)* *with its legal decrees and demands which was in force and stood against us (hostile to us). This [note with its regulations, decrees, and demands] He set aside and clearedcompletely out of our way by nailing it to [His] cross. [God] disarmed the principalities and powers that were ranged against us and made a bold display and public example of them, in triumphing over them in Him and in it [the cross]. **

2Corinthians 5:21 *God made him who had no sin to be sin for us, so that in him we might become the righteousness of God.*

Romans 6:23 The Amplified Bible *For the wages which sin pays is death, but the [bountiful] free gift of God is eternal life through (in union with) Jesus Christ our Lord.*

John 3:3 The Amplified Bible *Jesus answered him, I assure you, most solemnly I tell you, that unless a person is born again (anew, from above), he cannot ever see (know, be acquainted with, and experience) the kingdom of God.*

Ephesians 2:8-9 *For it is by grace you have been saved, through faith—and this is not from yourselves, it is the gift of God—not by works, so that no one can boast.*

Authority Over Nations – These passages of scripture will reveal to you how important it is for us to legislate authority over nations. God wants to be Lord over us, our land, regions, spheres, and nations. When he is head and revered in nations, he can bless it like he desired to when he placed Adam and Eve in the garden. **(*Study Genesis 1-3, Leviticus 26:21-39*)**

Revelation 2:26 *To all who are victorious, who obey me to the very end, To them I will give authority over all the nations.* *

Jeremiah 1:10 *Today I give you authority over nations and kingdoms to uproot and to pull down, to destroy and to overthrow, to build and to plant.* *

Isaiah 55:11 *So shall my word be that goeth forth out of my mouth: it shall not return unto me void, but it shall accomplish that which I please, and it shall prosper in the thing whereto I sent it.*

Romans 13:1-2 *Let every soul be subject to the governing authorities. For there is no authority except from God, and the authorities that exist are appointed by God. Therefore whoever resists the authority resists the ordinance of God, and those who resist will bring judgment on themselves.*

Proverbs 21:1 *The king's heart is in the hand of the LORD, Like the rivers of water; He turns it wherever He wishes.*

Isaiah 40:9-15 *O Zion, You who bring good tidings, Get up into the high mountain; O Jerusalem, You who bring good* *tidings, Lift up your voice with strength, Lift it up, be not afraid; Say to the cities of Judah, "Behold your God!" Behold, the Lord GOD shall come with a strong hand, And His arm shall rule for Him; Behold, His reward is with Him, And His work before Him. He will feed His flock like a shepherd; He will gather the lambs with His arm, And carry them in His bosom, And gently lead those who are with young. Who has measured the waters in the hollow of His hand, measured heaven with a span and calculated the dust of the earth in a measure? Weighed the mountains in scales and the hills in a balance? Who has directed the Spirit of the LORD, Or as His counselor has taught Him? With whom did He take counsel, and who instructed Him, And taught Him in the path of justice? Who taught Him knowledge, and showed Him the way of understanding? Behold, the nations are as a drop in a bucket, and are counted as the small dust on the scales; look, He lifts up the isles as a very little thing. **

Daniel 2:37 *You, O king, are a king of kings. For the God of heaven has given you a kingdom, power, strength, and glory.*

Isaiah 10:5-7 *Woe to Assyria, the rod of My anger and the staff in whose hand is My indignation. I will send him against an ungodly nation, and against the people of My wrath I will give him charge, To seize the spoil, to take the prey, and to tread them down like the mire of the streets. Yet he does not mean so, nor does his heart think so; But it is in his heart to destroy, and cut off not a few nations.*

John 19:10-11 *Then Pilate said to Him, "Are You not speaking to me? Do You not know that I have power to crucify You, and power to release You?" Jesus answered, "You could have no power at all against Me unless it had been given you from above. Therefore the one who delivered Me to you has the greater sin."*

Exodus 14:13-14 *And Moses said to the people, "Do not be afraid. Stand still, and see the salvation of the LORD, which He will accomplish for you today. For the Egyptians whom you see today, you shall see again no more forever. The LORD will fight for you, and you shall hold your peace.'*

Exodus 23:22 *But if you indeed obey His voice and do all that I speak, then I will be an enemy to your enemies and an adversary to your adversaries.*

Ezra 1:1-5 *Now in the first year of Cyrus king of Persia, that the word of the LORD by the mouth of Jeremiah might be fulfilled, the LORD stirred up the spirit of Cyrus king of Persia, so that he made a proclamation throughout all his kingdom, and also put it in writing, saying, Thus says Cyrus king of Persia: All the kingdoms of the earth the LORD God of heaven has given me. And He has commanded me to build Him a house at Jerusalem which is in Judah. Who is among you of all His people? May his God be with him, and let him go up to Jerusalem which is in Judah, and build the house of the LORD God of Israel (He is God), which is in Jerusalem. And whoever is left in any place where he dwells, let the men of his place help* *him with silver and gold, with goods and livestock, besides the freewill offerings for the house of God which is in Jerusalem. Then the heads of the fathers' houses of Judah and Benjamin, and the priests and the Levites, with all whose spirits God had moved, arose to go up and build the house of the LORD which is in Jerusalem.*

Daniel 2:20-21 *Daniel answered and said: "Blessed be the name of God forever and ever, for wisdom and might are His. And He changes the times and the seasons; He removes kings and raises up kings; He gives wisdom to the wise and knowledge to those who have understanding.*

Daniel 4:17 *This decision is by the decree of the watchers, and the sentence by the word of the holy ones, in order that the living may know That the Most High rules in the kingdom of men, gives it to whomever He will, and sets over it the lowest of men."*

Acts 17:26 *And He has made from one blood every nation of men to dwell on all the face of the earth, and has determined their preappointed times and the boundaries of their dwellings,*

Exodus 23:27-30 *I will send My fear before you, I will cause confusion among all the people to whom you come, and will make all your enemies turn their backs to you. And I will send hornets before you, which shall drive out the Hivite, the Canaanite, and the Hittite from before you. I will not drive them out from before you in one year, lest the land become desolate and the beasts of the field become too* *numerous for you. Little by little I will drive them out from before you, until you have increased, and you inherit the land.*

Govern Over Nations - Ask God for revelation of how to govern over nations because he gives direction for us to be victorious. He guides us in demonstrating dominion. You are not alone and do not have to be intimidated in being an inheritor and gatekeeper of nations. God will do mighty exploits through you for his glory. ***(Study Obadiah 1)***

2Chronicles 7:14 *If my people, which are called by my name, shall humble themselves, and pray, and seek my face, and turn from their wicked ways; then will I hear from heaven, and will forgive their sin, and will heal their land.**

Numbers 33:50-53 *Now the LORD spoke to Moses in the plains of Moab by the Jordan, across from Jericho, saying, "Speak to the children of Israel, and say to them: "When you have crossed the Jordan into the land of Canaan, then you shall drive out all the inhabitants of the land from before you, destroy all their engraved stones, destroy all their molded images, and demolish all their high places; you shall dispossess the inhabitants of the land and dwell in it, for I have given you the land to possess. **

Deuteronomy 8:18 *And you shall remember the LORD your God, for it is He who gives you power to get wealth, that He may establish His covenant which He swore to your fathers, as it is this day. **

Psalm 121:4 *Behold, He who keeps Israel shall neither slumber nor sleep. **

Deuteronomy 2:4-5 *And command the people, saying, "You are about to pass through the territory of your brethren, the descendants of Esau, who live in Seir; and they will be afraid of you. Therefore watch yourselves carefully. Do not meddle with them, for I will not give you any of their land, no, not so much as one footstep, because I have given Mount Seir to Esau as a possession.*

Deuteronomy 2:12 *The Horites formerly dwelt in Seir, but the descendants of Esau dispossessed them and destroyed them from before them, and dwelt in their place, just as Israel did to the land of their possession which the LORD gave them.)*

Deuteronomy 7:7-8 *The LORD did not set His love on you nor choose you because you were more in number than any other people, for you were the least of all peoples; but because the LORD loves you, and because He would keep the oath which He swore to your fathers, the LORD has brought you out with a mighty hand, and redeemed you from the house of bondage, from the hand of Pharaoh king of Egypt.*

Deuteronomy 20:1-4 *When you go out to battle against your enemies, and see horses and chariots and people more numerous than you, do not be afraid of them; for the LORD your God is with you, who brought you up from the land of Egypt. So it shall be, when you are on the verge of battle,* *that the priest shall approach and speak to the people. And he shall say to them, 'Hear, O Israel: Today you are on the verge of battle with your enemies. Do not let your heart faint, do not be afraid, and do not tremble or be terrified because of them; for the LORD your God is He who goes with you, to fight for you against your enemies, to save you.' **

Deuteronomy 28:7-12 *"The LORD will cause your enemies who rise against you to be defeated before your face; they shall come out against you one way and flee before you seven ways. "The LORD will command the blessing on you in your storehouses and in all to which you set your hand, and He will bless you in the land which the LORD your God is giving you. 'The LORD will establish you as a holy people to Himself, just as He has sworn to you, if you keep the commandments of the LORD your God and walk in His ways. Then all peoples of the earth shall see that you are called by the name of the LORD, and they shall be afraid of you. And the LORD will grant you plenty of goods, in the fruit of your body, in the increase of your livestock, and in the produce of your ground, in the land of which the LORD swore to your fathers to give you. The LORD will open to you His good treasure, the heavens, to give the rain to your land in its season, and to bless all the work of your hand. You shall lend to many nations, but you shall not borrow.*

Deuteronomy 32:7-8 *Remember the days of old, consider the years of many generations. Ask your father, and he will show you; Your elders, and they will tell you: When the*

Most High divided their inheritance to the nations, when He separated the sons of Adam, he set the boundaries of the peoples according to the number of the children of Israel.

Judges 9:22-24 *After Abimelech had reigned over Israel three years, God sent a spirit of ill will between Abimelech and the men of Shechem; and the men of Shechem dealt treacherously with Abimelech, that the crime done to the seventy sons of Jerubbaal might be settled and their blood be laid on Abimelech their brother, who killed them, and on the men of Shechem, who aided him in the killing of his brothers.*

1Kings 22:19-22 *Then Micaiah said, 'Therefore hear the word of the LORD: I saw the LORD sitting on His throne, and all the host of heaven standing by, on His right hand and on His left. And the LORD said, 'Who will persuade Ahab to go up, that he may fall at Ramoth Gilead?' So one spoke in this manner, and another spoke in that manner. Then a spirit came forward and stood before the LORD, and said, 'I will persuade him.'The LORD said to him, 'In what way?' So he said, 'I will go out and be a lying spirit in the mouth of all his prophets. And the LORD said, 'You shall persuade him, and also prevail. Go out and do so.*

Governing Over Principalities – Kingdom prayers and divine workings regarding your purpose and destiny must be established and conducted above principalities, such that it subdues, pushes back, or overthrows principalities in regions, spheres, and nations. **(*Luke 10:19, Ephesians 6:12*)**

Psalm 2:1-5 *Why do the nations rage, And the people plot a vain thing? The kings of the earth set themselves, **a**nd the rulers take counsel together, **a**gainst the LORD and against His Anointed, saying, "Let us break Their bonds in pieces **a**nd cast away Their cords from us." He who sits in the heavens shall laugh; The Lord shall hold them in derision. Then He shall speak to them in His wrath, And distress them in His deep displeasure.*

Psalm 149:6-9 *Let the high praises of God be in their throats and a two-edged sword in their hands, To wreak vengeance upon the nations and chastisement upon the peoples, To bind their kings with chains, and their nobles with fetters of iron, To execute upon them the judgment written. He [the Lord] is the honor of all His saints. Praise the Lord! (Hallelujah!)* *

Colossians 2:13-15 *And you, being dead in your sins and the uncircumcision of your flesh, hath he quickened together with him, having forgiven you all trespasses; Blotting out the handwriting of ordinances that was against us, which was contrary to us, and took it out of the way, nailing it to his cross; And having spoiled principalities and powers, he made a shew of them openly, triumphing over them in it.* *

Isaiah 44:28 *Who says of Cyrus, 'He is My shepherd, and he shall perform all My pleasure, saying to Jerusalem, "You shall be built," and to the temple, "Your foundation* *shall be laid."*

Isaiah 45:7 *I form the light and create darkness, I make peace and create calamity; I, the LORD, do all these things.'*

Ezekiel 5:12 *One-third of you shall die of the pestilence, and be consumed with famine in your midst; and one-third shall fall by the sword all around you; and I will scatter another third to all the winds, and I will draw out a sword after them.*

Daniel 4:35 *All the inhabitants of the earth are reputed as nothing; He does according to His will in the army of heaven and among the inhabitants of the earth. No one can restrain His hand or say to Him, "What have You done?"*

Amos 9:9 *For surely I will command, and will sift the house of Israel among all nations, as grain is sifted in a sieve; Yet not the smallest grain shall fall to the ground.*

1Corinthians 15:25-28 *For He must reign till He has put all enemies under His feet. The last enemy that will be destroyed is death. For "He has put all things under His feet." But when He says "all things are put under Him," it is evident that He who put all things under Him is excepted. Now when all things are made subject to Him, then the Son Himself will also be subject to Him who put all things under Him, that God may be all in all.*

Colossians 2:10 *And you are complete in Him, who is the head of all principality and power.*

Be Balanced In Governing Your Time Of Prayer, Your Personal - Generational - Regional Gates, Your Spheres Of Influence & Your Remnant (***Study Exodus 32***)

It will be important to have balance in seeking God while also being in position to release and govern what he grants to your hands. This is vital in making sure you safeguard the work and the people you are shepherding, equipping, and governing. In ***Exodus 32***, Moses was on the mountain hanging out with God, while the Israelites were making a golden calf. God told him to get off the mountain and go tend to the people because they were sinning. Proximity to what we build, the spheres we gatekeep, and the people we are to impact is essential to sustaining process and progress. When left unattended, the enemy will sift what we are legislating; people will also be left to erred propensities that open doors to sin against God.

Exodus 32:1-4 *And when the people saw that Moses delayed to come down out of the mount, the people gathered themselves together unto Aaron, and said unto him, Up, make us gods, which shall go before us; for as for this Moses, the man that brought us up out of the land of Egypt, we wot not what is become of him. And Aaron said unto them, Break off the golden earrings, which are in the ears of your wives, of your sons, and of your daughters, and bring them unto me. And all the people brake off the golden earrings which were in their ears, and brought them* *unto Aaron. And he received them at their hand, and fashioned it with a graving tool, after he had made it a molten calf: and they said, These be thy gods, O Israel, which brought thee up out of the land of Egypt.*

Exodus 32:7-9 *And the LORD said unto Moses, Go, get thee down; for thy people, which thou broughtest out of the land of Egypt, have corrupted themselves: They have turned aside quickly out of the way which I commanded them: they have made them a molten calf, and have worshipped it, and have sacrificed thereunto, and said, These be thy gods, O Israel, which have brought thee up out of the land of Egypt. And the LORD said unto Moses, I have seen this people, and, behold, it is a stiffnecked people.* *

This scripture also reveals knowing the remnant you are called to, where they are in their walk with God, and having responsible and mature leadership in place who can lead and legislate in your stead. The Israelites were prone to backsliding and rebellion. God called them stiff necked.

Stiffneck in Hebrew is *qâšeh* in Hebrew and means:

1. severe (in various applications)
2. churlish, cruel, grievous, hard (hearted), thing), heavy, impudent, obstinate, prevailed, rough(-ly), sore, sorrowful, stiff (necked), in trouble
3. roughly, obstinate, hard, difficult, severe
4. fierce, intense, vehement, stubborn, stiff of neck, stiff-necked
5. rigorous (of battle)

The Israelites did not know God for themselves and had a difficult time regarding the sovereignty of God. They knew God for what he could do but not who he was. When there were no performances or feeding of their desires and needs, they resorted to desiring what was familiar, common, and idolatrous. Aaron was a major leader who was called to aid Moses in leading the Israelites to the promised land. But without the guidance of Moses, he catered to the influences and desires of the people. Leadership should be equipped to govern like you govern. They should be able to lead the people in the ways of the Lord when you are not present. Do not leave your inheritance in the hands of people who are not equipped.

This is also essential when gatekeeping the wall of prayer, intercession, and spiritual warfare. Do not leave your regions and spheres in the hands of people who are fickle in prayer, pray for what God can do and not who he is, lack faith, are not loyal to you or to God, do not understand or regard the vision, purposes, guidance, and proceeding revelations of the prayer mandate, lack fervency or perseverance in prayer. Such people will expose your prayer wall, while exposing it to the enemy. The enemy will reclaim ground and territory that you have worked hard to maintain.

1Thessalonians 5:16-18 The Amplified Bible *Rejoice always and delight in your faith; be unceasing and persistent in prayer; in every situation [no matter what the circumstances] be thankful and continually give thanks to God; for this is the will of God for you in Christ Jesus.* *

Ephesians 6:18 *With all prayer and petition pray [with specific requests] at all times [on every occasion and in every season] in the Spirit, and with this in view, stay alert with all perseverance and petition [interceding in prayer] for all God's people. **

Colossians 4:2 The Amplified Bible *Be persistent and devoted to prayer, being alert and focused in your prayer life with an attitude of thanksgiving. **

Philippians 4:4-7 The Amplified Bible *Rejoice in the Lord always [delight, take pleasure in Him]; again I will say, rejoice! Let your gentle spirit [your graciousness, unselfishness, mercy, tolerance, and patience] be known to all people. The Lord is near. Do not be anxious or worried about anything, but in everything [every circumstance and situation] by prayer and petition with thanksgiving, continue to make your [specific] requests known to God. And the peace of God [that peace which reassures the heart, that peace] which transcends all understanding, [that peace which] stands guard over your hearts and your minds in Christ Jesus [is yours]. **

Acts 1:12-13 The Amplified Bible *Then the disciples returned to Jerusalem from the mount called Olivet (Olive Grove), which is near Jerusalem, [only] a Sabbath day's journey (less than one mile) away. When they had entered the city, they went upstairs to the upper room where they were staying [indefinitely]; that is, Peter, and John and [his brother] James, and Andrew, Philip and Thomas, Bartholomew (Nathanael) and Matthew, James the son of*

Alphaeus, and Simon the Zealot, and Judas (Thaddaeus) the son of James. All these with one mind and one purpose were continually devoting themselves to prayer, [waiting together] along with the women, and Mary the mother of Jesus, and with His brothers.

Acts 2:41-42 *So then, those who accepted his message were baptized; and on that day about 3,000 souls were added [to the body of believers]. They were continually and faithfully devoting themselves to the instruction of the apostles, and to fellowship, to eating meals together and to prayers.*

1Peter 5:8-12 *Be sober [well balanced and self-disciplined], be alert and cautious at all times. That enemy of yours, the devil, prowls around like a roaring lion [fiercely hungry], seeking someone to devour. But resist him, be firm in your faith [against his attack—rooted, established, immovable], knowing that the same experiences of suffering are being experienced by your brothers and sisters throughout the world. [You do not suffer alone.] After you have suffered for a little while, the God of all grace [who imparts His blessing and favor], who called you to His own eternal glory in Christ, will Himself complete, confirm, strengthen, and establish you [making you what you ought to be]. To Him be dominion (power, authority, sovereignty) forever and ever. Amen.* *

Proverbs 12:24 *The hand of the diligent shall bear rule: but the slothful shall be under tribute.*

2Peter 1:10 *Wherefore the rather, brethren, give diligence to make your calling and election sure: for if ye do these things, ye shall never fall.*

Being in proximity and in consistent prayer agreement with those who labor in prayer, opens you up to divine intel and revelation on how to govern in prayer. This principle will work for you if you work it.

Psalm 133:1-3 *How good and pleasant it is when God's people live together in unity! It is like precious oil poured on the head, running down on the beard, running down on Aaron's beard, down on the collar of his robe. It is as if the dew of Hermon were falling on Mount Zion. For there the Lord bestows his blessing, even life forevermore.*

I have been set under a few prayer warriors and received evident impartations from their prayer mantles. I have also listened to many prayer warriors and learned from their authority and governances of prayer. People have set under my mentorship and have matured in their ability to ascend, discern, navigate with precision and vision, legislate, rule, reign, tread, overthrow, succeed, and sustain in prayer. I have countless testimonies of how myself and others who I mentor will share a prayer request or concern with me, and because I partnered in agreement or they came under my governance, they saw immediate breakthrough.

Matthew 18:20 *For where two or three are gathered together in my name, there am I in the midst of them.* *

Matthew 18:19 *Again I say unto you, That if two of you shall agree on earth as touching any thing that they shall ask, it shall be done for them of my Father which is in heaven.* *

1Thessalonians 5:11 *Wherefore comfort yourselves together, and edify one another, even as also ye do.*

James 5:13-16 *Is anyone among you sick? Let them call the elders of the church to pray over them and anoint them with oil in the name of the Lord. And the prayer offered in faith will make the sick person well; the Lord will raise them up. If they have sinned, they will be forgiven. Confess your faults one to another, and pray one for another, that ye may be healed. The effectual fervent prayer of a righteous man availeth much.* *

2Chronicles 7:14 *If my people, which are called by my name, shall humble themselves, and pray, and seek my face, and turn from their wicked ways; then will I hear from heaven, and will forgive their sin, and will heal their land.*

Govern Through God's Presence & The Guidance Of Holy Spirit - God's presence is required in leading you, guiding you, identifying you as his, distinguishing you from all others, and demonstrating his kingdom works through you. Pursue his favored glory and live through it, such that you know how to navigate, work in, through, and with, his tangible weighty glory. Do not do anything without his leadership and his glory.

Exodus 33:14-23 The Amplified Bible *And the LORD said, "My presence shall go with you, and I will give you rest [by bringing you and the people into the promised land]." And Moses said to Him, "If Your presence does not go [with me], do not lead us up from here. For how then can it be known that Your people and I have found favor in Your sight? Is it not by Your going with us, so that we are distinguished, Your people and I, from all the [other] people on the face of the earth?"*

*The LORD said to Moses, "I will also do this thing that you have asked; for you have found favor (lovingkindness, mercy) in My sight and I have known you [personally] by name." Then Moses said, "Please, show me Your glory!" And God said, "I will make all My goodness pass before you, and I will proclaim the Name of the LORD before you; for I will be gracious to whom I will be gracious, and will show compassion (lovingkindness) on whom I will show compassion." But He said, "You cannot see My face, for no man shall see Me and live!" Then the LORD said, "Behold, there is a place beside Me, and you shall stand there on the rock; and while My glory is passing by, I will put you in a cleft of the rock and protectively cover you with My hand until I have passed by. Then I will take away My hand and you shall see My back; but My face shall not be seen." **

John 14:15-17 *If you love me, keep my commandments. I will ask the Father to give you another Helper, to be with you always. He is the Spirit of truth, whom the world cannot receive, because it neither sees him nor recognizes* *him. But you recognize him, because he lives with you and will be in you.*

John 14:26 *But the Helper, the Holy Spirit, whom the Father will send in my name, will teach you all things and remind you of everything that I have told you.*

John 16:13 *Howbeit when he, the Spirit of truth, is come, he will guide you into all truth: for he shall not speak of himself; but whatsoever he shall hear, that shall he speak: and he will shew you things to come.* *

Govern Using Angelic Assistance - Invite the angels to come gatekeep, govern, minister, do life and destiny with you.

Psalm 91:11 *For he shall give his angels charge over thee, to keep thee in all thy ways.* *

Hebrews 1:14 *Are they not all ministering spirits, sent forth to minister for them who shall be heirs of salvation?* *

Psalm 103:20 *Bless the LORD, ye his angels, that excel in strength, that do his commandments, hearkening unto the voice of his word.* *

Psalm 34:7 *The angel of the LORD encampeth round about them that fear him, and delivereth them.* *

1Chronicles 21:15 *And God sent an angel to Jerusalem to destroy it. As he was destroying, the LORD looked and relented of the disaster, and said to the angel who was destroying, "It is enough; now restrain your hand." And* *the angel of the LORD stood by the threshing floor of Ornan the Jebusite.*

FAITH AS A FORTIFIED HOUSE

- Faith is about aligning with who God is not what we want him to do. Not based on capability but the truth of his identity and supreme position as God, in that he knows what is best.

- God's perfect will entails what he has ordained for you to do and be before the foundation of the earth. Many times, we equate the fruit of our permissive will as God blessing us. God's permissive will entails your plans that God may bless through his Grace or that may provide fruit because of the goals, plans, and principles you utilize to ensure success.

- Being built up as a fortified house of faith is vital in being able to govern the divine intel her gives you. It is also essential to being a representation of faith that he has called you to be as a governer in your sphere of influence. It will be essential to lives these keys in this chapter as a lifestyle such that you do destiny with God as a son of God and as a serious business entreprenuer who embodies and lives sovereign in covenant relationship with God.

James 2:18-24 *Yea, a man may say, Thou hast faith, and I have works: shew me thy faith without thy works, and I will shew thee my faith by my works. Thou believest that there is one God; thou doest well: the devils also believe, and tremble. But wilt thou know, O vain man, that faith without works is dead? Was not Abraham our father justified by works, when he had offered Isaac his son upon the altar? Seest thou how faith wrought with his works, and by works was faith made perfect? And the scripture was fulfilled which saith, Abraham believed God, and it was* ***imputed*** *unto him for righteousness: and he was called the Friend of God. Ye see then how that by works a man is justified, and not by faith only.*

The Amplified Bible *What is the use (profit), my brethren, for anyone to profess to have faith if he has no [good] works [to show for it]? Can [such] faith save [his soul]? If a brother or sister is poorly* *clad and lacks food for each day, And one of you says to him, Good-bye! Keep [yourself] warm and well fed, without giving him the necessities for the body, what good does that do?*

So also faith, if it does not have works (deeds and actions of obedience to back it up), by itself is destitute of power (inoperative, dead). But someone will say [to you then], You [say you] have faith, and I have [good] works. Now you show me your [alleged] faith apart from any [good] works [if you can], and I by [good] works [of obedience] will show you my faith.

You believe that God is one; you do well. So do the demons believe and shudder [in terror and horror such as make a man's hair stand on end and contract the surface of his skin]! Are you willing to be shown [proof], you foolish (unproductive, spiritually deficient) fellow, that faith apart from [good] works is inactive and ineffective and worthless? Was not our forefather Abraham [shown to be] justified (made acceptable to God) by [his] works when he brought to the altar as an offering his [own] son Isaac?

You see that [his] faith was cooperating with his works, and [his] faith was completed and reached its supreme expression [when he implemented it] by [good] works. And [so] the Scripture was fulfilled that says, Abraham believed in (adhered to, trusted

> *in, and relied on) God, and this was accounted to him as righteousness (as conformity to God's will in thought and deed), and he was called God's friend. You see that a man is justified (pronounced righteous before God) through what he does and not alone through faith [through works of obedience as well as by what he believes].*

Let me express that part again, "*through works of obedience as well as by what he believes!*"

Many want to say they have faith, yet they lack obedience and necessary workings that justify what they speak. The scripture lets us know that faith is not just saying we believe God as even the devil believes in God. Even the devil has enough faith and common sense not to deny the existence of God and not to deny the ability of God. But that alone does not mean you are demonstrating faith. Faith requires works! Works that demonstrates your obedience unto the Lord.

Works is *ergō* in the Greek and means:

1. (to work); toil (as an effort or occupation)
2. by implication, an act: — deed, doing, labour, work
3. business, employment, that which any one is occupied, that which one undertakes to do, enterprise, undertaking
4. any product whatever, anything accomplished by hand, art, industry, or mind, an act, deed, thing done: the idea of working is emphasized in opp. to that which is less than work

There is no way to operate in faith and not work the vision of faith that God has given or to work in your relationship with God as you live in faith.

The definition lets us know that we are to toil and labor in our works of faith. It also reveals to us that faith is literally like a business, place of employment.

The definition uses the word "*enterprise*" to describe faith. *Enterprise* means "*a project that is undertaken or that is to be undertaken, especially one that is important or difficult or that requires boldness or energy.*"

Enterprising allows you to govern and impact others by the business of faith and destiny as a lifestyle with God.

As we work our business of faith, we are to operate in it as if we have taken on a project and in our case, it is a lifestyle project that releases the enterprising business of God. And as we consider the definition further, it is a lifestyle project that requires us to be bold and that we are assert energy.

Now when we consider taking on a project, that project is a scheme of specific task that has to be contemplated, devised, or planned. We have to contemplate and calculate the costs. Those costs are our time, finances, actions, people involved, etc. Yet because it is our project, we make the necessary sacrifices to complete our project.

- If no one else believes in it, we have to believe in it.

- If no one else invests time, energy, finances, etc. into it, we still have to invest time, energy, finances, etc. into it.
- If no one else cares, loves, or have passion and zeal for it, we have to still care, love, be passionate, and exhibit zeal for the project.
- If no one else wants to consistently work it and see it to completion, we have to remain consistent and see our project through to the end.

Faith is an honorable obligation!

It is our project, and we have to be dedicated to the vision at hand.

This is the same bold, energetic work that goes into faith.

James said these workings can be seen. It can be seen by the literally eye and yields evidence that you are walking in faith. Your faith should be a testimony that you have a personal relationship with God.

This passage of scripture references the faith of Abraham. Abraham had was asked by God to sacrifice his only son. Imagine having to sacrifice your child?

Despite how agonizing this must have felt, Abraham was obedient to God. He was faithful to his project and in the act of fulfilling it, God withstood his hand and had him sacrifice a ram instead. The scripture says that Abraham believed God and it was imputed unto righteousness.

One challenge the body of christ has is that often we think believing God is just a statement of faith, but if you study the definition of believe and even the scriptures, you will find that belief is a commitment. So, you cannot say you believe God, but your life is not committed to him. I cannot say I love hamburgers but every time someone offers me one, I turn it down or you never see me eating hamburgers. My actions have to be in alignment with what I say I believe.

Abraham did not just have lip service belief, he had committed belief and because of that, he was imputed unto righteousness.

Imputed is *dikaiosynē* in the Greek and means:

1. equity (of character or act); specially (Christian) justification: — righteousness
2. righteousness in a broad sense: state of him who is as he ought to be, righteousness, the condition acceptable to God (not to man, not to you, but to God)
3. the doctrine concerning the way in which man may attain a state approved of God
4. integrity, virtue, purity of life, rightness, correctness of thinking feeling, and acting
5. in a narrower sense, justice or the virtue which gives each his due

So imputed reveals and examines the character and deeds that you have invested in your walk of faith - your project of faith.

When a bank considers equity – what you have or put into an investment, it has to have value. Even the materials and resources you use, who did the work, who much time, energy, etc. was invested, whether you follow through with your what you said you were going to do or what you said you believed, etc., helps determine your equity value. If we consider that as it relates to being imputed unto righteousness, we cannot be investing negative characteristics and then acting like we have given righteous value to our faith walk.

Being imputed unto righteousness means that our equity has to exhibit "integrity, virtue, purity of life, rightness, correctness of thinking feeling, and acting" that is acceptable unto God – that God deems of good equity. Not what we feel we have invested as when the bank considers your equity, you can have one estimate of worth and they can have another. So, it you cannot determine your own equity of faith. Only God can do that. Only God can determine the justice or virtue that he feels you are due as you journey with him in faith.

And we all know that that journey has to align with his plan – the vision of faith he has provided for you. And know we know that that vision of faith has to possess his character of equity to truly be imputed as a working of faith.

Let them ponder on that a minute. Help us Lord Jesus!

As we consider the revelation on faith, let's consider some keys for SHIFTING into governing the visions and spheres of influence God has given you with unwavering faith.

- What is your vision of faith for that project – intel – visions - you are currently living out with God?

- Do you truly believe in the project – intel – visions - where you are not just stating that you believe but you are committed?

- Are you being obedient to God and what you contend you are committed to? How so? How not? What needs to align in your soul, heart, mind, actions to come into committed obedience?

- Can your commitment and obedience be seen to the natural eye? Can others see your faith in action? Is it evident that you believe and trust God? How so? What changes or improvements need to be made in your workings to demonstrate your faith?

- What does your faith look like behind the scenes? What does your faith look like when no one is watching? Is our faith and belief compromised? Are there litigations present where the enemy can accuse you, expose you as not being blameless in faith, or you character and righteousness compromised?

- As your faith walk evolves,

a. Are you committed to the project of faith?
b. Who has left or slacked in your faith journey?
c. Who is support you in your faith? What is your godly covenant relationship with them?
d. Who is committed to helping you see it through?
e. Who has or is investing in it? (time, resources, counsel, finances, etc.)
f. What is the project requiring of you and are you sacrificing to see it fully completed (time, resources, counsel, energy, finances, focus, etc.)
g. Which part of the project needs fresh zeal or more of your focus? How do you plan to make those changes to invest fully in the project of faith?

- Is there equity of character in what you are investing in your project of faith?
    a. Is this equity in alignment with God's character and nature?
    b. Is he pleased with your equity – meaning does he deem your character and nature and how you are handling your faith project of living as valuable?
    c. What areas need to be healed in your soul, heart and/or mind to improve your equity?
    d. What areas need to be transformed in your character and actions to increase the value of your equity?

- Check with God throughout your faith journey to make your he is pleased with your equity and make changes through his leading.

Verse 18-19 The Message Bible *I can already hear one of you agreeing by saying, "Sounds good. You take care of the faith department, I'll handle the works department." Not so fast. You can no more show me your works apart from your faith than I can show you my faith apart from my works. Faith and works, works and faith, fit together hand in glove.*

THE SPIRIT OF LITIGATION

Litigation entails a dispute over legal rights and obligations that can often be disputed in a court proceeding. Often when it comes to a situation, positioning, systematic proceeding, judicial matter, property or land dispute, legal matters of marriage, separation, or divorce, justice proceedings, legalities over children and/or bloodline matters, if the enemy cannot hinder a person from being victorious, he will look for legal ways in policies, procedures, or spiritual and natural principles, standards, and laws in effort to attack, delay, deny, frustrate, overthrow, thwart, or wreak havoc in a person's life. These litigations may be legal and have merit, but the enemy's main reason for using this tactic is to prosecute, charge, indict, sue, shame, scandal, disbar, terminate, dissolve, annul an agreement so that the person can no longer be successful or obtain occupancy of what God is releasing to them.

These efforts are also for the purposes of nullifying the jurisdiction to which God wants that person to govern with dominion in their lives, bloodline, regions, and/or spheres of influence. As the enemy is always seeking to have legal ground and claim to the lineages, territories, and spheres that God wants a person and their heritage to possess. Territorial governance is the greatest blessing a person can have because whoever owns the land and sphere has the greatest authority - kingly authority.

Sometimes the litigation can be spiritually illegal, but the enemy will use natural laws and procedures that are legal to challenge and attack a person. Spiritually, the person has not done anything wrong for the enemy to attack, so he will find a clause in a natural policy or procedure to attack a person. We will see this in employment, business, and marketplace endeavors, school and educational matters, business, and entrepreneurial dealings, economic and financial situations, and political proceedings. The enemy may also litigate natural policies, procedures, and/or laws of a company, worldly system, contract, binding agreement, or a moral position of integrity to attack a person's finances, character, progress, process, and success.

There are also instances where open doors of compromise, subtle, unrecognized, or unrepentant sins, disobedience and sin against the laws and standards of God can be used to assert litigations in areas of a person's life. Litigation comes for a person individually and generationally because it wants everything they have worked for with God. In the natural courts, people are sued and everything they have worked hard for can be stripped away from them in these legislated proceedings. The enemy seeks to operate in this manner in a spiritual litigation. Until the sin is repented of, and the doors of sin are closed, the enemy can assert litigation to attack a person. A sifting through attacks starts to take place to strip the person of their governance of sonship, destiny, blessings, and generational inheritance. The sifting especially occurs if they is no intercessor standing in the gap for others or a bloodline curse breaker.

Zechariah 3 :1-7 The Amplified Bible *Then the guiding angel showed me Joshua the high priest [representing disobedient, sinful Israel] standing before the Angel of the LORD, and Satan standing at Joshua's right hand to be his adversary and to accuse him. And the LORD said to Satan, "The LORD rebuke you, Satan! Even the LORD, who [now and ever] has chosen Jerusalem, rebuke you! Is this not a log snatched and rescued from the fire?" Now Joshua was clothed with filthy (nauseatingly vile) garments and was standing before the Angel [of the LORD]. He spoke to those who stood before Him, saying, "Remove the filthy garments from him." And He said to Joshua, "See, I have caused your wickedness to be taken away from you, and I will clothe and beautify you with rich robes [of forgiveness]." And I (Zechariah) said, "Let them put a clean turban on his head." So they put a clean turban on his head and clothed him with [rich] garments. And the Angel of the LORD stood by. And the Angel of the LORD [solemnly and earnestly] admonished Joshua, saying, "Thus says the LORD of hosts, 'If you will walk in My ways [that is, remain faithful] and perform My service, then you will also govern My house and have charge of My courts,* *and I will give you free access [to My presence] among these who are standing here.*

Satan is generally in the court of heaven using these litigations to contend against a person's life, prayers, promises, and prophecies. He wants to take back what God has said rightfully belongs to that person or to make the person look disqualified and/or illegal, such that what God is saying is theirs is taken. Handling these matters in the court of heaven, repenting when necessary to break any legal ground, while standing in the truth of God's promises, prophecies, and who he has purposed the person to be and do, are the greatest weapons against the spirit of litigation. Also, know that God will overthrow Satan for the person and all those attached to them, as we discern this in ***Zechariah 3***. God will not allow Satan to use these litigation proceedings to hinder a person's victory. It is important for the person to trust this truth as they walk out these types of experiences. God will prevail with restoration, restitution, and victory!

Isaiah 43:1-4 The Message Bible *But now, GOD's Message, the God who made you in the first place, Jacob, the One who got you started, Israel: "Don't be afraid, I've redeemed you. I've called your name. You're mine. When you're in over your head, I'll be there with you. When you're in rough waters, you will not go down. When you're between a rock and a hard place, it won't be a dead end— Because I am GOD, your personal God, The Holy of Israel, your Savior. I paid a huge price for you: all of Egypt, with rich Cush and Seba thrown in! That's how much you mean*

to me! That's how much I love you! I'd sell off the whole world to get you back, trade the creation just for you.
John 10:29-31 *And Jesus answered and said, Verily I say unto you, There is no man that hath left house, or brethren, or sisters, or father, or mother, or wife, or children, or lands, for my sake, and the gospel's, But he shall receive an hundredfold now in this time, houses, and brethren, and sisters, and mothers, and children, and lands, with persecutions; and in the world to come eternal life. But many that are first shall be last; and the last first.*

You can learn how to legislate in the courts of heaven in my manual, "*Gatekeeping Regions For God's Glory.*"

THE POWER OF BLAMELESSNESS

Power Of Blamelessness To Thwart Litigation

God continues to highlight being blameless as vital to keep of protection in this present season and beyond. Especially against litigations, for Scouts, gatekeepers, and leaders. In this season, the world and accusers may do everything in its power to point/accuse/charge the body of Christ. Despite their attempts, remain blameless, says the Lord.

Proverbs 28:18 *Whoever walks blamelessly is kept safe; but one with perverse ways will fall suddenly.*

Psalm 84:11 *For the LORD God is a sun and a shield. the LORD will give grace and glory. He withholds no good thing from those who walk blamelessly.*

Jesus presents us blameless.

Jesus did what no other man or law could do. He humbled himself and became man, for the purposes of posturing himself as the perfect sacrifice that could help us to become blameless. He came down from heaven, was born of woman, lived among mankind, demonstrated that man could walk blameless, preached the gospel with unwavering faith, was persecuted, was crucified such that his innocent blood was shed and sacrificed for the world's sins. He died on the cross then rose again with all power in his hands. Jesus' works restored us into right alignment of sonship with God, while paying all our sins and debts. We became blameless through his workings. He SHIFTED us into having the opportunity to live blameless as we continuously live in covenant relationship with God and evolve in Christlikeness with him.

Colossians 1:19-23 *For it pleased the Father that in him should all fulness dwell; And, having made peace through the blood of his cross, by him to reconcile all things unto himself; by him, I say, whether they be things in earth, or things in heaven. And you, that were sometime alienated and enemies in your mind by wicked works, yet now hath he reconciled In the body of his flesh through death, to present you holy and unblameable and unreproveable in his sight: If ye continue in the faith grounded and settled, and be not moved away from the hope of the gospel, which ye have heard, and which was preached to every creature which is under heaven; whereof I Paul am made a minister.*

Jude 1:24 *Now to him who is able to keep you from stumbling and to present you blameless before the presence of his glory with great joy.*

Ephesians 5:27-28 *That he might present it to himself a glorious church, not having spot, or wrinkle, or any such thing; but that it should be holy and without blemish. So that he might present the church to himself in splendor, without spot or wrinkle or any such thing, that she might be holy and without blemish.*

Malachi 3:1-3 *Behold, I will send my messenger, and he shall prepare the way before me: and the Lord, whom ye* *seek, shall suddenly come to his temple, even the messenger of the covenant, whom ye delight in: behold, he shall come, saith the LORD of hosts. But who may abide the day of his coming? and who shall stand when he appeareth? for he is like a refiner's fire, and like fullers' soap: And he shall sit as a refiner and purifier of silver: and he shall purify the sons of Levi, and purge them as gold and silver, that they may offer unto the LORD an offering in righteousness.*

- Oxford defines blameless as innocent of wrongdoing.

- The word *Blameless* in Greek is "*Anegklētos*" which means *unable to be called into account, unable to be corrupt, unreproveable, unaccused, unblemished, spotless innocent.*

    - *as a sacrifice without spot or blemish*
    - *morally: without blemish, faultless, unblameable*

Jesus was able to boast that there was nothing of Satan and the world in him. He was confident of this truth about himself.

John 14:30 *Hereafter I will not talk much with you: for the prince of this world cometh, and hath nothing in me.*

I believe the entire reason Jesus Christ was adamant about us receiving his Holy Spirit was so we could boast of this truth like he did. Holy Spirit embodies us with his presence, power, character, fruit, and ability to be guided into ALL truth about what within us need to be purged out so that we are blameless before God.

John 4:23-24 *But the hour cometh, and now is, when the true worshippers shall worship the Father in spirit and in truth: for the Father seeketh such to worship him. God is a Spirit: and they that worship him must worship him in spirit and in truth.*

John 8:31-32 *Then said Jesus to those Jews which believed on him, If ye continue in my word, then are ye my disciples indeed; And ye shall know the truth, and the truth shall make you free.*

John 14:15-25 *If ye love me, keep my commandments. And I will pray the Father, and he shall give you another Comforter, that he may abide with you for ever; Even the Spirit of truth; whom the world cannot receive, because it seeth him not, neither knoweth him: but ye know him; for he dwelleth with you, and shall be in you. I will not leave you comfortless: I will come to you. Yet a little while, and the world seeth me no more; but ye see me: because I live, ye shall live also. At that day ye shall know that I am in my Father, and ye in me, and I in you.*

He that hath my commandments, and keepeth them, he it is that loveth me: and he that loveth me shall be loved of my Father, and I will love him, and will manifest myself to him. Judas saith unto him, not Iscariot, Lord, how is it that thou wilt manifest thyself unto us, and not unto the world? Jesus answered and said unto him, If a man love me, he will keep my words: and my Father will love him, and we will come unto him, and make our abode with him. He that loveth me not keepeth not my sayings: and the word which ye hear is not mine, but the Father's which sent me. These things have I spoken unto you, being yet present with you. But the Comforter, which is the Holy Ghost, whom the Father will send in my name, he shall teach you all things, and bring all things to your remembrance, whatsoever I have said unto you.

John 16:13 *But when he, the Spirit of truth, comes, he will guide you into all the truth. He will not speak on his own; he will speak only what he hears, and he will tell you what is yet to come.*

John 16:33 *Howbeit when he, the Spirit of truth, is come, he will guide you into all truth: for he shall not speak of himself; but whatsoever he shall hear, that shall he speak: and he will shew you things to come.*

Truth is *alētheia* in Greek and means:

1. Verity (factual, true belief) - objectively what is true in any matter under consideration
2. truly, in truth, according to truth
3. of a truth, in reality, in fact, certainly what is true in things appertaining to God and the duties of man, moral and religious truth
4. in the greatest latitude the true notions of God which are open to human reason without his supernatural intervention

5. the truth as taught in the Christian religion, respecting God and the execution of his purposes through Christ, and respecting the duties of man, opposing alike to the superstitions of the Gentiles and the inventions of the Jews, and the corrupt opinions and precepts of false teachers even among Christians
6. truth as a personal excellence, that candor of mind which is free from affection, pretense, simulation, falsehood, deceit

Often times we want relief from the consequences of our sins, compromises, or inferences that reveal we do have something in common with Satan, but because we are still holding on to the hope of having our way, we have not fully embodied truth – fully received truth in our inward parts where not having nothing in common with Satan is our truth.

Psalm 51:6-17 *Behold, thou desirest truth in the inward parts: And in the hidden part thou shalt make me to know wisdom. Purge me with hyssop, and I shall be clean: Wash me, and I shall be whiter than snow. Make me to hear joy and gladness; That the bones which thou hast broken may rejoice. Make me to hear joy and gladness; that the bones which thou hast broken may rejoice. Hide thy face from my sins, and blot out all mine iniquities. Create in me a clean heart, O God; and renew a right spirit within me. Cast me not away from thy presence; and take not thy holy spirit from me. Restore unto me the joy of thy salvation; and uphold me with thy free spirit.*

Then will I teach transgressors thy ways; and sinners shall be converted unto thee. Deliver me from bloodguiltiness, O God, thou God of my salvation: and my tongue shall sing aloud of thy righteousness. O Lord, open thou my lips; and my mouth shall shew forth thy praise. For thou desirest not sacrifice; else would I give it: thou delightest not in burnt offering. The sacrifices of God are a broken spirit: a broken and a contrite heart, O God, thou wilt not despise.

If we are going to live blameless, we have to desire truth, WANT truth, seek truth, and embody truth wholeheartedly. No matter how much it hurts, makes us feel some type of way, strips us of our desires or will, we must want truth.

The inward parts – hidden parts - are those parts of us that we do not want people to know about or to touch. It is the secret parts of us that we keep hidden, safeguard, protect, hold dear.

We can even be calculated in how we engage people, God and his Holy Spirit where these areas of ourselves are not touched – they are held sacred – viewed as off limits – A NO NO!

We may even be quick to put people, God and his Holy Spirit in their place when they come with true for our inward part – our secret or most sacred treasures.

People, God and Holy Spirit know this is a sacred cow, so they do not even attempt to engage you regarding the inward parts of your life that needs truth. But God is saying that this is the part that satan will come for in this hour and seasons to come to erect blame upon us.

This is the part that Holy Spirit needs to be able to guide you, me, us, into ALL truth so truth can set us free. So that we can boast like Jesus – **NOTHING OF SATAN IS FOUND IN ME!**

HELP US HOLY SPIRIT!

Blamelessness takes humility, trusting God and what he reveals.

Blamelessness takes maturity!

Jesus Christ was the word of truth, so he was constantly being guided, washed, perfected by the word of truth. This is what we have to do as well. As Holy Spirit guide us into all truth, we must allow what he reveals to us personally and through the biblical word of God to purge us as hyssop – make us whiter than snow. All of this is being done through us surrendering to Holy Spirit and allowing truth to have its perfect work in us.

Hyssop is a form of medicine used for healing and religious purposes. Are you willing to allow truth to work like spiritual healing medicine on the inside of you?

The word of God waters, washes, discerns, corrects, divides what is of God and what is not of God, cuts out, chastises, does surgery, instills God's truth, will, and plan.

2Timothy 3:16 *All scripture is given by inspiration of God, and is profitable for doctrine, for reproof, for correction, for instruction in righteousness.*

Ephesians 5:26 *That he might sanctify and cleanse it with the washing of water by the word.*

John 17:17 *Jesus prays to His Father saying, "Sanctify them through thy truth: thy word is truth.*

Sanctify in the Greek *hagiazō* and means:

1. make holy, i.e. (ceremonially) purify or consecrate; (mentally) to venerate, hallow, be holy
2. to render or acknowledge, or to be venerable or hallow
3. to separate from profane things and dedicate to God
4. consecrate things to God, dedicate people to God
5. to purify, to cleanse externally, to purify by expiation
6. free from the guilt of sin, to purify internally by renewing of the soul

What are those secret things in your inward parts – hidden parts you hold dear that you need to allow the truth of the Holy Spirit to medicate where GOD sanctifies you with his word. Where God makes you HOLY through truth that sanctifies you by his word.

NOT YOU BUT GOD MAKING YOU HOLY THROUGH TRUTH!

This needs to be a constant self-exploration for now and seasons to come. This is THE daily bread self-examination that will nullify the litigations of the enemy.

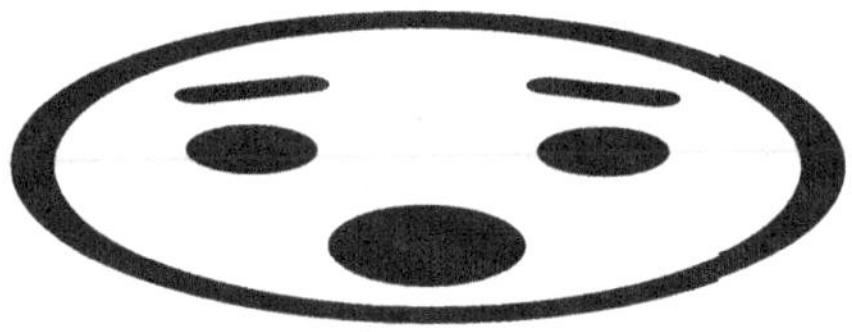

HELP US HOLY SPIRIT!

We want to get so broken to God doing his perfect work in us, that when the word comes, a quick work manifests that immediately closes the door to anyway the enemy can litigate us.

Hebrews 4:12 *For the word of God is quick, and powerful, and sharper than any two-edged sword, piercing even to the dividing asunder of soul and spirit, and of the joints and marrow, and is a discerner of the thoughts and intents of the heart.*

We need to allow the revelation that Holy Spirit gives us personally and through biblical scriptures to do the following:

- Use the word of God to divide what is of God in our lives from what is not of him.

- Use the word of God to extract what is not of God from our soul, heart, mind, body, and spirit.

- Use the word of God to overthrow every lie that the enemy uses to keep us bound to demons.

- Use the word of God to cut out any word, character trait, hurt, pain, and flaw that keeps us bound to demons.

- Spend time studying, meditating on, and soaking in the word of God so that it becomes physical truth in us.

- Allow God's word to go inside of our (heart, mind, soul, identity), and cleanse everything that is contrary to the word of God for our lives.

- Study and meditate on God's word and be refilled in his truth concerning our identity, purpose, destiny, and who he is as daddy God, Lord and savior, ruler and king of our lives.

As the word of truth works and lives in your, it will help you to make sure your good or what could be questioned as sin is not evil spoken. This is another way the enemy will come to try and litigate believers says the Lord.

Isaiah 5:20 *Woe to those who call evil good, and good evil.*

Romans 14:16-20 *Therefore do not let what is a good thing for you [because of your freedom to choose] be spoken of as evil [by someone else]; for the kingdom of God is not a matter of eating and drinking [what one likes], but of righteousness and peace and joy in the Holy Spirit. For the one who serves Christ in this way [recognizing that food choice is secondary] is acceptable to God and is approved by men. So then, let us pursue [with enthusiasm] the things which make for peace and the building up of one another [things which lead to spiritual growth]. Do not, for the sake of food, tear down the work of God. All things indeed are [ceremonially] clean, but they are wrong for the person who eats and offends [another's conscience in the process].*

Do not allow the accusations and demonic decrees released by the accuser cause you to stumble or to throw you off course says the Lord.

- Study and embody scriptures on being blameless.

- Ask God to reveal and deliver you from sin issues.

- Ask God to reveal areas to you where inferences can be made to question whether you are blameless. As God to reveal inferences to you, do not make excuses, justify, defend, negate, or ignore them.

Look for the legal ramifications in the spiritual realm through his biblical word, standards, and laws. Study these revelations and cleanse yourself of any sins, propensities, perceptions, mindsets, ideologies, and character flaws that would disregard or make excuses for these inferences.

Ask him to show you how litigation can operate through these situations. Do what he says to close doors to inferences and judge litigation operations in the court room of heaven. Keep these doors closed in your personal and generational lines to further deter litigation. This is so vital to making sure you do not become relaxed in this area.

Songs Of Solomon 2:15 *Take us the foxes, the little foxes, that spoil the vines: for our vines have tender grapes.*

The Amplified Bible *Catch the foxes for us, the little foxes that spoil and ruin the vineyards [of love], While our vineyards are in blossom.*

Scriptures On Blamelessness

Genesis 17:1-3 *When Abram was ninety-nine years old, the LORD appeared to him and said, "I am God Almighty; Walk [habitually] before Me [with integrity, knowing that you are always in My presence], and be blameless and complete [in obedience to Me]. "I will establish My covenant (everlasting promise) between Me and you, And I will multiply you exceedingly [through your descendants]."*

Then Abram fell on his face [in worship], and God spoke with him, saying.

Proverbs 10:9 *He who walks blamelessly walks surely, but he who perverts his ways will be found out.*

Perverted means to "*twist, knot, distort, make or be crooked, prove perverse, declare perverse.*"
It is so important not to twist godly principles or the truth itself where you are not able to discern what you are doing and how it misaligns you with God.

Proverbs 11:5 *The righteousness of the blameless will direct his way, but the wicked shall fall by his own wickedness.*

Proverbs 11:20 *Those who are perverse in heart are an abomination to the LORD, but those whose ways are blameless are his delight.*

God delights in us being blameless. It pleases him, while posturing us in a content and safe position of sonship.

Proverbs 28:10 *Whoever causes the upright to go astray in an evil way, he will fall into his own trap; but the blameless will inherit good.*

Our lack of blamelessness impacts others. It can cause them to stumble and be led astray from God. We must take our impact on others seriously. Especially in this hour where God is requiring us to be key storehouse representations of him that governs lives and spheres for his glory.

Psalm 101:2 *I will be careful to live a blameless life. When will you come to me? I will walk within my house with a blameless heart.*

Revelation 14:5 *In their mouth was found no lie, for they are blameless.*

Psalm 15:2 *He who walks blamelessly does what is right, and speaks truth in his heart.*

Wow, I love this scripture. What does it look like when your heart has a voice, and that voice speaks truth? We must want truth in our inward parts. We also must recognize that out of the heart, the mouth speaks. Your heart will reveal whether you are blameless or not. Especially, when what you are speaking is not aligning with God or his biblical word. Make a conscious effort to examine what your heart is saying. Be honest when there are inferences that open the door to litigation. Being honest with yourself and what is a heart matter is vital to your posture to remain blameless.

Psalm 119:80 *Let my heart be blameless toward your decrees, that I may not be disappointed.*

Psalm 18:23 *I was also blameless with him. I kept myself from my iniquity.*

Psalm 119:1 *Blessed are those whose ways are blameless, who walk according to the LORD's law.*

Titus 1:6 *If anyone is blameless, the husband of one wife, having children who believe, who are not accused of loose or unruly behavior.*

Titus 1:7 *For the overseer must be blameless, as God's steward; not self-pleasing, not easily angered, not given to wine, not violent, not greedy for dishonest gain.*

As leaders, we are held to a higher standard. We are to be essential representations of blamelessness, demonstrating that we honor God, his biblical laws, and standards. We must covenant to one mate, raising godly seeds, and possessing behavior that is in alignment with his character, nature, and identity.

Commissioning Prophetic Word Regarding Becoming Blameless
By: Minister Mercedes Carr

There is a high cost to blamelessness because it is a high calling. Though the cost is humility, the seat of blamelessness is the seat of the high calling. A seat that I myself had to take says the Lord. Not everyone will come into right standing with blamelessness. It takes a yielded heart and a divine surrender. It takes an eternal laying down of everything that is enthroned on your heart. You have been summoned, commissioned, and called to the seat of blamelessness. You are an heir of righteousness. This is your heavenly inheritance. This is your birthright. Anything less is mediocre and below heavens standard. As you bow, come up higher to the seat of blamelessness. Come up higher to the seat of the high calling. Live here, dwell here, be transformed and eternally shifted here.

Phillipians 1:20-22 *I eagerly expect and hope that I will in no way be ashamed, but will have sufficient courage so that now as always Christ will be exalted in my body, whether by life or by death. For to me, to live is Christ and to die is gain. If I am to go on living in the body, this will mean fruitful labor for me. Yet what shall I choose? I do not know!*

If we do not die, someone else will.

God is calling us to choose ye this day and pick the hill we are to die on.

"*The hill you die on*" is a military phrase.

Hill to die on (plural hills to die on) (idiomatic) is a posture to pursue with wholehearted conviction and/or single-minded focus, with little or no regard to the cost.

An allusion to the military practice of capturing/holding a hill (high ground), no matter the cost or (lack of) benefit.

Live In The Shift!

RESOURCES

Taquetta Baker's Manuals

Deliverance Is The Children's Bread Volume I
Deliverance From The Stronghold Of Suicide
Fivefold Operations Volume I
Gatekeeping Regions For God's Glory
Unmasking The Power Of The Scouts Volume I
Unmasking The Power Of The Scouts: Soul Stealers Volume II

Websites

Blueletterbible.com
Biblestudytools.com
Dictionary.com
Olivetree.com
Strong's Exhaustive Bible Concordance Online
Bible Study Tools

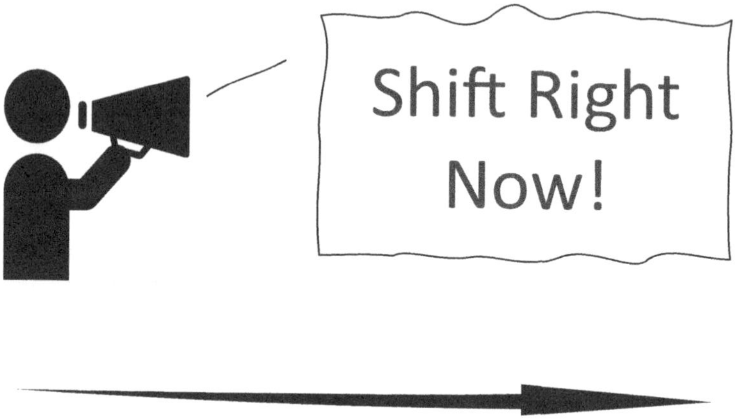
Shift Right
Now!

Be a Healthy You!

Kingdom Shifters Product Line

Products available at kingdomshiftingbooks.com and amazon.com	
Books (Paperback, Kindle, and e-books available)	
Healing the Wounded Leader	There is an App for That
Apostolic Governing	Sustaining The Vision Workbook
Apostolic Mantle	Annihilating Church Hurt
Healing the Wounded Leader	Discerning the Voice of God
Release the Vision	Feasting in His Presence
Birthing Books That Shift Generations	Prayers that Shift Atmospheres
Atmosphere Changes (Weaponry)	Dismantling Homosexuality
Strategies for Eradicating Racism	Let There Be Sight
Kingdom Shifters Decree That Thang	Kingdom Watchman Builder on the Wall
Kingdom Heirs Decree That Thang	Kingdom Keys to Governing Relationships
Fivefold Operations – Manuals I, II, and III	Unmasking the Power of the Scouts – Volumes I and II
Processing Grief & Loss	Cultivating Destiny From The Womb
Kingdom Wellness Counseling & Mentoring Manual I	Deliverance From The Stronghold of Suicide

Truth About Willful Sin	Ascending Into Heavenly Realms
Gatekeeping Regions For God's Glory	KW Life Coaching Manual
The Power Of Purity	Deliverance Is The Children's Bread Volume I & II
Books for Liturgical / Interpretive Dance Ministries	
Dance & Fivefold Ministry	Dance from Heaven to Earth
Spirits that Attack Dance Ministers	Dancers! Dancers! Dancers! Decree That Thang
CD's	
Decree That Thang	Kingdom Heirs Decree That Thang
Teaching and Worship	

Made in the USA
Columbia, SC
10 March 2024

32970434R00108